Your Ever Growing Income:

The Rising Yield on Investments

"US Edition"

Henry Mah, CMA

Disclaimer

The information and opinions in this book must not be considered investment advice. The information is intended to be for informational purposes only. I am not an investment advisor and I am not recommending any security or investment product.

Opinions offered here can never be a substitution for independent analysis and due diligence. The book may contain some forward-looking statements and opinions on subject matter that is familiar and already well-covered. Your guess as to the future value of any security is as good as mine, or that of a broker. Forecasting is an unreliable enterprise.

There are always risks involved with investing and investors must expect occasional losses on the risk they take. It is certain there will be periods of time when all investing strategies, including dividend growth investing, will underperform the market. It is always best to have measured expectations when approaching investing in any form.

I dedicate this book to my lifelong partner, Raelene, my son Troy, daughter Theresa, her husband Alain, our grandkids Gabby and Sam and my sister Alice.

To Tom Connolly, I'm grateful for allowing me to borrow so many of his thoughts and ideas for this book.

Special thanks to Theresa, Alain and Sam for their help with editing and the cover artwork.

Table of Contents

Foreword

When Henry asked me to prepare a few words by way of a foreword for his great new book, I was in the middle of tallying up our 2018 dividends. It is something we do every November: detail our yearly dividend increases. It does not take long: I hold five stocks, my wife six and the dividend changes have already been recorded by hand as they occur during the year on a wee chart up on the tack board in the laundry room. (There are columns for: buy date, number of shares and price; original yield and dividend; and yield on cost. We change the dividend and yield on cost when it occurs.) Each time my wife's dividends increase; I get taken out to lunch.

This year, though, we are most excited. One of our stocks, Bank of Nova Scotia (BNS), is approaching 100%. One hundred percent of what? When we purchased our BNS in 1990, the dividend was 25¢ a share. Now they send us $3.40 dividend per share every year. Now for the magic of dividend growth; Henry's book will explain it for you in very simple terms. You've heard of stock splits, perhaps. Splits occur every 10 to 15 years on quality growth stocks. Anyway, since 1990 our BNS has had two, 2:1 split. So, our original price of $14.56, when divided by 4 begets $3.64. On the other side of the coin, our original 200 shares became 400 shares on the first 2:1 split and 800 shares on the second 2:1 split. Look at things this way. We paid $3.64 for our shares and these shares now pay us $3.40 in dividends. We are just about receiving the full amount we paid for the shares back each year (it is actually 93.4%) by way of dividends. Most folks do not know that quality stocks become safer as companies build wealth. AND, and, this is a very important 'and', our 200 shares are now 800 shares (with the splits) and the current price is somewhere close to $70 per share. Does this seem a bit complicated? It's not. It's wonderful! Our income from BNS has grown (to $2,720 a year) and our capital has grown (to $56,000). It is growth that builds these returns; good companies grow: They grow their earnings, they deploy retained earnings properly and they grow their dividends. Learn how this all works from Henry's book and share in the wealth. Henry is convincing; he knows his material well and he employs good examples.

As you are most likely just beginning with dividend growth, some of what you encounter may have to be taken on faith for a while. It is truly unbelievable. This happened to me when I first encountered dividend growth in a 1984, Letter to the Editor of the *Financial Times*. Over the years though, our faith has been confirmed with real cash flow. Hold for it!

*Here is how the BNS steadily grew over the years from 1990: .25, .25, .26, .28, .29, .31, .33, .36, .55, .66, .76 in 2000, .87, .96, .98, $1.10, 1.32, 1.50, 1.74, 1.92, 1.96, 1.96 again in 2010, $2.05, 2.19, 2.39, 2.56, 2.72, 2.88, 3.05, 3.28, and now in 2018, .85 quarterly x 4 = $3.40 a year. We are living the dream . . . building wealth through dividend increases, which, in concert with well deployed retained earnings, drive capital gains in a commensurate amount. I've never, ever, seen a fund increase their distributions like this. Build your own portfolio, with Henry's help.

TOM CONNOLLY
Publisher of: *The Connolly Report* since 1981
www.dividendgrowth.ca

Preface:

Before we get started, I'd like to highlight a few items that you should keep in mind when reading through my book:

1. I am not an academic and, therefore, there will be no past analytical data, forecasting or comparisons to other strategies.
2. I do not present any charts on how well one might do with this strategy or assumptions on potential earnings.
3. I don't provide sample portfolios or lists of recommended stocks.
4. Every effort will be made to provide you with clear and precise steps on the strategy I propose.
5. Some of the numbers used in my examples and charts may not reflect current figures when you read the book, but the points I'm trying to make are still valid.
6. I apologize for some of the fuzzy charts, they lose their resolution when condensed in size.
7. Examples provided are from accounts I am familiar with and represent real numbers.
8. Examples presented are not a guarantee of similar success in the future, but as real-world results of practicing the process I recommend.
9. Some examples given are from Canadian accounts, US stocks performed better during the period 2007 to 2018. One could assume US stocks will have shown better results.
10. There will be no reference to current market value throughout the book, such as: "This portfolio is now worth... $" or "We have beat the market by... % over the past... years".

11. This book will present and explain a process for you to follow. Much of the information will detail a step-by-step process much like a workbook or exercise book.
12. I will try to avoid recommending individual stocks, instead I'll provide you with the task of evaluating the stocks on your own with a set of guidelines, showing you how to gather the data, how to analyze the data (as best I can) and allow you to decide whether a stock qualifies.
13. Once you have established your own list of stocks following my process, you can repeat the process on different stocks or indexes if you wish.
14. The process will not become outdated over time. The status of the companies may change, but the process will continue to screen out those which do not meet your requirements.

Now, onwards and upwards, as they say!

The No Win Scenario: The Market Kobayashi Maru!

If you're a science fiction buff like I am, you will be familiar with the Kobayashi Maru scenario from Star Trek. In its construction, the Kobayashi Maru is a no-win scenario. James T. Kirk was the only one to ever beat the Kobayashi Maru — by reprogramming the simulation so that it was possible to win. Clever filmmaking, but also a very clever lesson used by many to illustrate a very important point. The only way to win a no-win scenario is to change the rules, or simply don't play their game.

I believe to a certain extent that trying to beat the market, relying on market timing and depending on market returns is a bit like a no-win scenario, or trying to beat the house in a casino. You win via luck, you lose by design.

I am offering you a solution to the Market Kobayashi Maru with:

- A philosophy that beats the "sleight of hand" of market timing.
- A system that eliminates the "best guess" way of stock picking.
- An evaluation system which is simple, effective and allows you to quickly identify quality stocks.
- An alternative to seeking market returns and eliminating the reliance on market returns.
- A system where your returns are not tied to price fluctuations and won't play a part in your investment decisions.

Don't play their game, play yours.

With this book, we are not going to play the price game. Certainly, the goal is to purchase stocks, keeping in mind there are no guarantees in investing, just as there are no guarantees in life. But we'll change the game so that it works to your benefit by providing you with results that are measured, not by price or the direction of the market, but with you having greater control over your returns, where you will be able to see those returns grow.

We're not going to play their game of needing to beat the market, rather, we'll play our own game, with our own rules, ignoring the market altogether!

Introduction:

Income growth is not a difficult concept to grasp, and there is no doubt that it is important, but the topic is rarely mentioned-- even in prominent publications. (Tom Connolly, *The Connolly Report*, Dec. 1994)

Why should you listen to me or take my advice? You shouldn't!

What I hope you will do is take the time to read the book in its entirety, it's not long, and decide if it might be a strategy suitable for you. I don't want you to take anyone's suggestions or advice point blank. You need to determine your personal investing goals. Nothing replaces due diligence and research, even with the strategy that I propose.

"73.6% of all statistics are made up"- Business Insider

"85% of statistics are false or misleading"- World Science Festival

I think it's important to stress the trouble with statistics. There is always "more than one way to skin a cat", as they say, just as there are many ways to achieve one's goal from investing. Some investors like the excitement of daily trading, others do extensive research, charting and forecasting, some believe in Passive Exchange Traded Funds (ETF), and there are those who feel owning everything in every market produces superior results. Don't rely too heavily on other's achievements, tips, stats, "inside information". I have always found the only truth is that some strategies are easy, others complex, some work some of the time, but none work all of the time.

Whether you are a new or a seasoned investor, you may find investing overwhelming. What to buy, when, how much, which markets, who to listen to and finally, when you do buy, and have you made a good choice?

I'll address these questions and suggest an investing strategy from a different viewpoint than most:

- Instead of concentrating on capital appreciation (price of your stocks rising), we will focus on the income your stocks generate.
- Instead of comparing your returns to market indexes or other common benchmarks, we will measure your income growth.
- Instead of worrying about being fully diversified (spreading your investments "across the board"), we will concentrate on selecting a few of the best stocks.
- Instead of providing you with a list of recommended stocks or sample portfolios, **you** will learn to evaluate the stocks and decide which best suits your needs.

In this book I will be demonstrating a method of finding stocks, stock evaluation, and then suggest the best way to make these stocks generate the most income.

- You won't be constantly looking for new stocks to buy.
- You won't need to jump on the latest "hot" stock (like Facebook or the "cannabis craze").
- You won't be monitoring the price of your stocks, worrying when the market changes direction or be concerned should the value of your portfolio drop.
- You won't have to wait until the end of the year to see how your investment strategy is working. You will receive confirmation updates each month or quarter.
- You will, over time, learn to ignore stock prices and market fluctuations.

What exactly am I proposing? Well, quite simply, the following quote from *The Connolly Report*, (a bi-monthly publication on dividend growth investing, published since 1981) describes it best:

"If a company does not pay a dividend, don't buy it. If it doesn't grow the dividend don't buy it either."

That's basically it! It didn't strike home with me immediately, but every time I thought about investing in a particular stock, I kept going back to that simple statement and asking the question, does it pay a dividend and has the dividend grown?

The more I looked into dividends and dividend growth investing, the more sense it made. As I began to understand the strategy and the unique method of stock evaluation, the more convinced I became that dividend growth investing was the way to go.

The Connolly Report evaluates stocks by yield, Graham Value, cyclically adjusted price-to-earnings ratio, and compound annual growth rate. Tom Connolly presents a list of stocks which meet his criteria for the benefit of his subscribers, so they can determine which stocks are expensive (to buy) and compare the different evaluation methods to assist in determining value (a reasonable price to buy). These are great tools and information and have gained Tom a lot of followers and admirers.

I will present a slightly different approach than Connolly's, one where you will evaluate and select which stocks to add to your own portfolio. It's not a fill-in-the-blank, or do-what-I-say strategy, but one where we will provide you with a process to follow but you will do the footwork and come to your own conclusions. You won't need to study company financial statements, project future earnings or perform any other complicated and extensive analysis. I'll present you with a simple, straight-forward and easy method of evaluating and screening out stocks. Our goal is not to find the most stocks, but a select few which will help you achieve a clear and obtainable objective: to provide you with a **growing income from your investments.**

One final note, most of the financial examples used in the book come from accounts I am personally familiar with, with real numbers and achievable results and not fictional projections.

Chapter 1

Since the market value in most cases has depended primarily upon the dividend rate, the latter could be held responsible for nearly all the gains realized by investors. (Security Analysis, by Graham, Dodd & Cottle)

Breaking away from the norm:

I think one of the hardest parts of investing is trying to decide how and which advice, because most seems quite sensible, to apply to your own investment strategy:

- Invest in yourself first.
- Stocks are primarily a long-term investment.
- Avoid High Yield Stocks.
- Only make investments you understand.
- Learn from the mistakes of others.
- Consider the level of risk you can accept.
- Keep your investment fees low.

You've probably heard these and many more, most are valid, others sound reasonable but don't really pertain to your particular situation, or leave you wondering how to implement what they advise.

So what might make investing simpler and practical for you? After many years of playing the market and reading a number of published materials on various investment strategies, I have found that investing for income and concentrating on income growth is the best, most risk-free way to utilize the market. We're not giving up on capital appreciation, just ignoring the constant monitoring of the market's ups and downs.

Every day the financial news announces the markets' movement. On Bloomberg and the CNBC News channel, the current price of each stock scrolls across the screen providing updates of their current price and how much the price is up or down for the day. The news anchor and others may have opinions on what's causing the change, and some will provide projections or recommendations on the latest best buys or what to avoid. Even CBS Sunday Morning, one of my favorite shows, displays the week's closing market changes.

The problem with all the news and financial advice is that it's all centered on the changes in the market, the price of stocks and the short-term changes of those stock prices. Whatever happened to investing for the long-term? No wonder the majority of investors panic if the market drops 300 points or more.

If you own shares of a company stock and are wary of constant monitoring of the market and its volatility, what's the alternative?

Income is the alternative!

The stock producing the income is worth more as the income it produces increases. (Lowell Miller, *The Single Best Investment*)

So, how do we stop watching the price of stocks or caring if the market is up or down? One of the easiest methods is to change the way you think about your investments and what you expect from them.

When one considers a Certificate of Deposit (CD) or bond it's the interest rate that's important. In fact, most people will shop around to find the best or highest interest rate available and after they've bought they forget about the purchase. The main reason people buy CDs or bonds is because they know they will get back their original capital (investment) plus the interest. But, the problem is that the interest is fixed, meaning it stays the same. We said we want a growing income and that we can achieve that goal by investing in stocks which pay and grow their dividend (what I refer to as income).

Apply the same thinking to the stocks you are considering as you would if they were CDs, but substitute income for interest rate. Ask yourself, how much income your investments are going to return, **but also ask the question, will your income grow**?

With this book I would like to convince you that it's not that difficult to concentrate on the concept of "income" and show you how it becomes much easier over time.

Once you are ready to change the way you think about your stocks, we also want to replace the word "price" with "income" and make that your focus. For example, instead of wondering if your stock price(s) are up, check to see if your income is up, and disregard price altogether. It's not that price isn't important, it's just that one should not make it the key focus of your attention. Realize you will be holding your stocks for the long-term. The goal is to find good investments, then give them time to grow the income, which will then, in turn, grow the price.

However, even the staunchest dividend supporters have difficulty getting away from watching price. How often have you heard or read the following comment; "You are getting paid while you wait".

Every time I read or hear someone making that statement, I think, wait for what? What else could they mean but for prices to go up! Even those thinking about income and possibly aware of its benefit are stuck in the same rut, always watching price. Let's see if I can help change that.

Why income?

- Income will make your investment choices easier,
- You will mostly invest in large, stable and profitable companies,
- You will see your income grow each month or quarter,
- Your growing income will also grow the stock price,
- Your income will not be affected by market fluctuations, and
- You will learn to ignore the daily changes in share price and market changes.

To illustrate how income investing works, I will use a real-world example. My wife bought shares of a bank stock for our grandson in 2007 and invested the following amounts:

2007	$ 5,555	(market peak)
2008	$ 500	(financial crisis)
2009	$ 500	(financial crisis)
2011	$ 1,000	(start of recovery)
2017	$ 1,000	(10 years later)
	$ 8,555	(total investment)

The following chart shows the income they received and the income growth rate for each year:

2008	$217.30	
2009	$253.81	16.80%
2010	$281.43	10.88%
2011	$323.94	15.10%
2012	$379.31	17.09%
2013	$431.32	13.71%
2014	$481.32	11.59%
2015	$531.84	10.50%
2016	$588.67	10.69%
2017	$655.52	11.36%
2018	$767.36	17.06%
	$4,911.82	(income received and reinvested)

Look at the income each year and how consistent the income growth is each year. Money was not added every year, yet the income continued to grow by at least 10%, over the previous year, regardless of the market fluctuations during that period. Had she put the money in a CD, at 1% or even 2%, during those years of low rates, how much income would they have received over the 11 years? At such a low rate of return, not much, as well there would have been no real income growth. In our case, by concentrating on income, the income grew in 11 years from $217.30 to $767.36, or 253.13%!

I will provide another example. My wife (the better stock picker) bought this stock in 2008, at a market high, added funds for a few years and has ignored the stock since 2011.

2007	$ 37	(bought one share)
2008	$10,000	(initial purchase in Jan 08)
2008	$ 5,000	(invested at a high price)
2010	$ 2,500	(added funds)
2011	$ 2,000	(last purchase)
	$19,537	(total investment)

Here's the income she received each year and the annual income growth rate:

2008	$ 286.88	(no pymt 2 Qtr 2008)
2009	$ 634.17	121.06%
2010	$ 788.03	24.26%
2011	$ 936.85	18.89%
2012	$1,066.76	13.87%
2013	$1,159.46	8.69%
2014	$1,257.04	8.42%
2015	$1,398.84	11.28%
2016	$1,584.02	13.24%
2017	$1,813.84	14.51%
2018	$2,091.42	12.30%
	$13,017.31	(income received & reinvested)

This example shows that my wife has gotten 67% of her initial investment back, just from the income she's received ($13,017/ $19,537) x 100 = 67%. As for income growth, from 2009 (first full year of income) to 2018, the income grew from $634.17/year to $2,091.42/year or 229.79%.

She's essentially being "paid" while she waits, but not for the stock price to rise, but rather, for her next income payment to increase.

In both examples most of the investment in the stocks were made before the financial crisis (meaning we paid a high price for the stocks before the market dropped in 2009), but they have averaged 10% income growth each year and above. Even with severe market fluctuations, the benefits of income growth investing are real and substantial. Remember, with income investing we are not watching the price of the stocks, but the income those stocks provide.

And this is what I want you to understand. By investing in "income-earning" stocks (which I will discuss later in this book), you will see your income grow each year regardless of how much you invest, whether the market is up or down, even if you stop adding funds to your holdings. Of course, your income will grow faster the more you invest, but the ultimate goal is always income growth. Did I forget to mention price? No, because our eyes are on the income.

So, are you ready? Let's get started.

Chapter 2

Do not save what is left after spending, but spend what is left after saving. (Warren Buffett, Chairman and CEO, Berkshire Hathaway)

The first step:

Before one can generate income, one must begin saving money. The savings do not have to be large, in the beginning, but should be made on a regular basis and increase as one earns more. Whether you start saving $50 a month or $1,000 a month, saving as a priority is the beginning of any successful investment strategy. You must save money to make money and the more you save the more you make.

A great philosophy for saving is to not think about it, instead, make it a routine!

I also suggest you reduce your debt and avoid any payments where excessive interest is being charged, such as credit cards. A Loan Consolidation is one way to reduce the cost of interest, **provided you don't start adding additional debt**.

There are some excellent books and reference sources available to help people to reduce debt and cut expenses, probably better advice than I can provide (consider "How not to move back in with your parents: the young person's complete guide to financial empowerment", by Rob Carrick). Regardless of your current financial health, one must make the effort to save and then not touch your investment money, even for short-term needs.

Let's get back to business, once you have decided you are ready to start saving you may be ready to start investing.

Many beginner investors put their money into High Interest Savings accounts or CDs, and that's fine, **but don't consider savings and investments as the same thing.** Everyone should have a cash reserve, savings and even possibly insurance which might be used to cover unexpected expenses. But your investments should be considered future money**, a Retirement Time Capsule** if you will, which should not be touched until you need it in retirement.

Whether you start investing at age 20 or 60 will not affect the strategy I propose. What will change is how you choose to invest (I will discuss the choices later in the book) and of course, the amounts you can invest. Obviously, someone starting at 20 years old will not have large amounts to invest but does have the advantage of time, time for their investments to grow and compound. Someone who starts later, even as late as 60 years old, will need to invest larger amounts and have a shorter timeline before they will begin to draw down funds. Still, even 10 years can provide significant income from a large portfolio of income producing stocks, as I'll demonstrate later in the book.

If you are not investing for income, then it is fair to analyze or ask, what they expect of their savings during retirement. Is it a guaranteed fixed income, their capital to be secure, perhaps just the ability to sell a portion of the capital to meet their needs (the 4% withdrawal is often suggested)? And of course, they hope not to outlive their money. But how often have you heard someone say, "I want to enjoy my retirement while I can and die broke"? Too many in my experience.

The sad part is that many might get their wish, by finding during their retirement years they must cut expenses and curb their lifestyle to make ends meet. Nothing is more stressful in retirement then feeling you might outlive your financial resources!

I'd prefer to have my investments generate an ever-growing income stream, one which continues to grow, especially during retirement, while I'm drawing down funds.

It is important to remember that when interest rates dropped during the financial crisis of 2008-2009, so did the interest paid on fixed income (CDs and Bonds). In fact, they almost dropped to zero. The value of stocks fell as well, so those depending upon selling shares and fixed income to meet their daily expenses found they had little or no protection and most likely suffered profound losses. Luckily, during that period and after several years of low interest rates, inflation remained at 1.5% to 2%. Small comfort.

Inflation: up, up and up!

Inflation is a rise in the general level of prices of goods and services in an economy over a period of time. When the general price level rises, each unit of currency buys fewer goods and services. Consequently, inflation also reflects an erosion in the purchasing power of money – a loss of real value in the internal medium of exchange and unit of account in the economy. A chief measure of price inflation is the inflation rate, the annualized percentage change in a general price index normally the Consumer Price Index over time.

Source Microtrends. Data sourced from 1914 → 2018

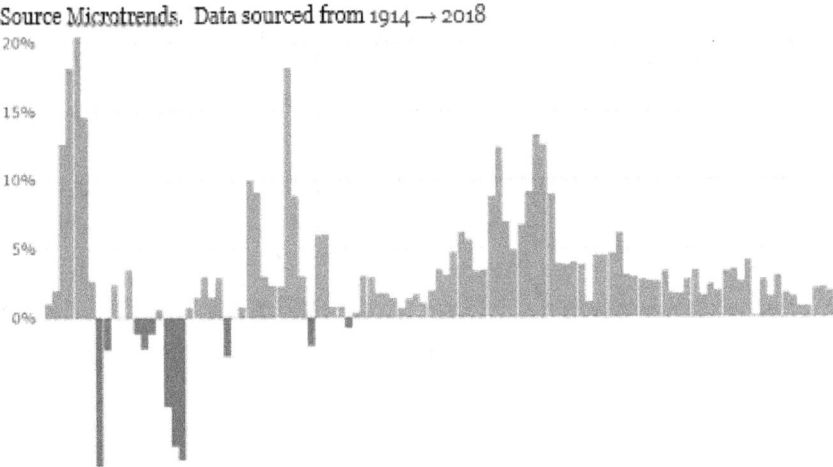

Since 1914 through 2018, the US inflation rate dropped only twelve times, but for every other year the price of goods and services has increased. The last time inflation dropped was 1954. The graph is misleading, because the increases in inflation compound every year. This means that what cost a dollar one year, cost more the next and even more the next. The average inflation rate since 1914 has been 2.9% per year, meaning prices double every 25 years. I always question those figures because many essential items seem to increase much faster than the reported rate of increase.

Year	US Inflation Rate
1998	1.60%
1999	2.70%
2000	3.40%
2001	1.60%
2002	2.40%
2003	1.90%
2004	3.30%
2005	3.40%
2006	2.50%
2007	4.10%
2008	0.01%
2009	2.70%
2010	1.50%
2011	3.00%
2012	1.70%
2013	1.50%
2014	0.80%
2015	0.70%
2016	2.10%
2017	2.10%
2018	1.90%

In the Lee Child novels his character, Jack Reacher, often says, "Hope for the best, but plan for the worst". Apply that rule to inflation and hope that inflation remains low or below average, but plan for much higher inflation and costs.

Ultimately this is my goal, to recommend a way for your investments to provide a growing stream of income to offset rising costs. Not a "pie in the sky" or "jackpot at the end of a rainbow" goal, but a simple method where you see the results of your efforts as time goes on and feel confident that your **"Retirement Time Capsule"** will meet your future income needs.

Visionary

Most people don't consider themselves as visionary: "thinking about or planning the future with imagination or wisdom".

I think you have the opportunity to become a visionary about your financial future, but thinking or planning about it won't get you there. One has to work to achieve their dreams and I believe the Income Growth investment strategy can help make your dreams a reality.

Chapter 3

A careful selection of a few investments having regard to…their potential intrinsic value over a period of years ahead and…a steadfast holding of these fairly large units through thick and thin. (John Maynard Keynes, British Economist, creator of Keynesian economics)

Getting schooled:

Once you've started saving for your future, I suggest the next step is to develop an investment strategy. Here you have lots of choices, but where to start and which to choose? Do I start buying stocks and try to sell when they rise 15%? Do I follow Jim Cramer and his recommended picks? Do I buy a group of Exchange Traded Funds (ETF) and hope for market returns, or do I try to figure out how to start a Value or Growth portfolio because my ultimate goal is to beat the market return? That's the problem many investors face and, unfortunately, the majority will lose money trying to make guesswork their market strategy. Yes, money can be made, it has been done, but those that succeed will often be a small minority.

The Income Investment Strategy:

Dividend paying ability, in the long run, determines value. (Arnold Bernhard, founder of Value Line).

Income investing could be considered the flip side of "growing the pile" (having the value of your investments go up). Most investors consider the combination of capital appreciation (stocks going up in price) and dividends (see Definitions) as their total return. However, too many consider dividends as the minor contributor of the two.

I believe the exact opposite. I believe that dividends (what I refer to as income), especially a growing dividend, is the driver that generates price growth and, in the end, contributes to a more sustainable return.

A dividend is derived from a company's earnings. If a company is growing its earnings and paying out an ever-higher amount in dividends, eventually investors will recognize the value of those higher dividends and begin buying the shares. Subsequently, the price of those shares will rise.

Investing for income (dividends) means you will look for companies that pay you dividends for buying and holding their shares. **To achieve a growing income, the company should increase the dividend over time, thereby providing you with more income for each share you own, and not requiring you to sell shares to receive the higher income.**

Your income will be generated from holding "individual" stocks, not a bundle (i.e. Exchange Traded Funds) which will most likely include mediocre stocks. My strategy works when you hold only quality equities with at least 10 years of positive growing earnings and a history of passing along a percentage of those earnings to the shareholder.

To better illustrate what I call "the income-growth game", I'll compare it to playing golf:

- You don't hit the longest ball but will always be down the middle and in the fairway.
- You don't make headlines for great shots but will continue to play steadily and dependably.
- You probably won't get the occasional Eagle but will consistently get pars and birdies, finding your

handicap gradually improving (your income rising).

- You won't be recognized as the #1 player but you will almost always be in the top 10.

I hope that these kinds of odds are ones you are interested in playing. It's not often you truly get exposed to a "sure thing", but in investing, quality dividend growth stocks come as close as you can get!

Why not just buy an ETF?

Bullet-proof, dividend paying common stocks with a record of sustained payout growth should be the core investment asset class for income-oriented investors. (Don Coxe, Basic Points, Sept. 2011)

ETFs (Exchange Traded Funds) are fast becoming the choice of many investors. They are a way to have a diversified portfolio of stocks or bonds in a single investment and can be traded just like a stock. The fees are low and they offer vast diversification, a way to "cover all the bases", if you will. Some suggest that if you own around five ETFs you'll cover the entire US, Canadian, Emerging and International markets. However, the five largest ETF Providers offer **1,929** US ETFs (as of June 28, 2018), with many new ETFs coming out almost weekly. Considering that ETFs can contain hundreds, if not thousands of individual stocks, it is no longer a simple choice, is it?

Let me say that there is no best method to invest and ETFs may be a reasonable choice for those who have set market returns as their objective. But, from an "income" perspective, I do have a few objections to them, mainly because:

- They hold too many stocks, the good, bad and in-between,
- The distribution (Income) rarely grows or grows at a slow rate,
- The distribution may include dividends, Return of Capital, and Capital Gains, misleading investors who assume the distribution is all dividends,
- Although ETFs initial fees may appear to be low, the more you invest the higher the fees become,
- You have no control over the stocks chosen or their weighting within the ETF (for example, one stock may be 3.5%, while another .05%),
- The fund needs to trade (constant buying and selling) to rebalance,
- If you were to evaluate all the stocks in a single ETF, you would most likely find many of them to be poor or mediocre income producing stocks, and
- Most ETFs try to match the performance to the market or Index they represent. Since the financial crisis of 2008, the market has generally been on an upswing. But I do wonder how ETFs will do during the next major correction or extended sideways market. Personally, I do not think they will do well.

Remember, that if our objective is long-term income growth, you will find that ETFs don't provide the income growth that individual stocks do. I will be explaining further and support my hesitation to recommend ETFs with some facts when I provide my stock evaluation process.

As for the various other investment choices, they are all dependent on price and the market, which is what we are attempting to avoid.

Which stocks and where to find them?

Investors should remain focused on high-quality investments such as strong dividend-paying stocks and use volatility to their advantage. (David Rosenberg, Journalist, *Financial Post*)

If you've read other investing books, you may wonder how anyone could simplify the process of selecting and evaluating stocks. Well, you are in for a surprise, because by applying my strategy of income investing ideas to the US market, I found it to be so simple I wonder why everyone does not do it.

I have already mentioned that I like dividend-paying stocks, and in the United States there are many to choose from. One could look at companies in the Russell 3000 (3000 of the biggest US companies), the S&P 500 (500 large-cap companies), or the Dow 30 (30 largest companies). Sounds like a lot of companies and work, but there is an easier way. There is a select group of 57 companies that have raised their dividend for 25+ years, called the Dividend Aristocrats (see Appendix A).

As income growth is our objective it is to our advantage to refer to the Dividend Aristocrats as it is made up of the best dividend (income) payers of the group mentioned. But just because these 57 companies have paid and raised their dividend for 25+ years, does not make them equal. We will look closer at the 57 companies, to see if some raise their dividend by the bare minimum each year or have others provided higher returns. I want to sort through the 57 Dividend Aristocrats and find those companies which not just pay a dividend, but grow the dividend at a reasonably high rate.

The companies you may find most suitable, by following my method, may not be the fastest growing, highest flyers, but should provide you with a steady stream of income and, most importantly, grow that income as time goes on. My strategy is not flashy, nor is it about getting rich quickly, rather to generate a reliable source of income so you can ignore market fluctuation and share price. ***But, Income investing is more than just a growing dividend, which we discuss later.***

Excel worksheets:

Before we evaluate each of the 57 Dividend Aristocrat stocks, I want to suggest, if you are not already familiar with Excel, I hope you will explore using it, or at least a similar program.

Besides providing more information than what your broker (from whom you purchase stocks) offers, it is a very efficient method to observe greater detail on your holdings. Excel also performs many calculations easily, such as calculating the 95% dividend growth rate or the 10-year average dividend yield of each stock, the adjusted cost base (average cost) of each stock, the annual dividend income growth, current yield and yield on your total investment percentages and growth, all of which we will discuss later.

I should point out that a disadvantage of Excel is that you need to cross-check your data to ensure the numbers and report balances shown in Excel are correct. You should always check your Excel balance and number of shares with your broker's account balances. But even with its limitations, Excel will enable you to design specific reports to provide the information you wish or would like to see, I feel strongly any investment strategy benefits from diligent data tracking.

Whatever method you use, I feel you will begin to look forward to tracking your progress.

I have provided a downloadable package of Excel worksheets at the link below:

https://drive.google.com/drive/u/1/folders/1kD-ZtK7WkIINobzB3HYJ1tnwnh9P3NDf

The download will include the following worksheet (formulas included), where you'll record your evaluation results for each stock and add useful comments. This tracking is an integral part of an income growth investment strategy.

Company	Symbol /Yield	Payout Ratio	2008	2009	2010	2011	2012	2013	2014	2015	2016	2017	Div Gth 10 Yr
AbbVie Inc.	ABBV												
Percentage Growth													
Abbott Laboratories	ABT												
Percentage Growth													
Archer-Daniels-Midland	ADM												
Percentage Growth													
Automatic Data Proc.	ADP												
Percentage Growth													
AFLAC Incorporated	AFL												
Percentage Growth													
A.O. Smith Corporation	AOS												
Percentage Growth													
Air Products and Chem	APD												
Percentage Growth													

I'll describe what the headings are and where to find the information, in the next section.

So, let's get started and "sort the wheat from the chaff".

Jumping the stocks through the hoops:

Know what you own and know why you own it. (Peter Lynch, manager of the Magellan Fund)

To sort through the 57 Dividend Aristocrat companies and determine which might provide you with the best income I've trimmed my stock selection to three simple rules.

The Three Guiding Rules

1. Has the dividend grown over the past 10 years by at least 95%?
2. Has the dividend growth for the past five years been 5% or more per year?
3. Is the current yield of the stock above 1%?

When you find a stock meeting the three rules add the company to a new list, which I like to call your **"List of Stocks to Consider".** This list is intended to be your "buy" list. I emphasize the word "consider", as this list needs to be flexible and monitored periodically, it is likely to change over time.

Just as your list need to be flexible, the application of these guiding rules needs to be flexible as well. Many may feel that rules are not meant to be broken, but there are valid exceptions, and I'd like you to remember, **if you are not flexible you risk becoming outdated**.

To illustrate my point, let's look at three different "exception" scenarios when evaluating the Dividend Aristocrats:

1. **A company has paid and raised their dividend for 25 years, but the dividend growth is less than 95%.**

This is an example of an exception because there are companies, like utilities or the "Dividend Kings", companies which have raised their dividend for 50 years and may not be on the Aristocrats list. I like to call some of them the "Steady Eddies". Many of them post a 5% dividend increase over 10 years which provides a 63% dividend growth, below our 95%, but you may still consider them an attractive stock choice.

One must also remember that there are many contributing factors that affect dividend growth rates. For instance, because of the financial crisis and low interest rates, dividend growth rates have slowed for many companies. This kind of fluctuation should not necessarily cancel a good long-time performing stock from your list. Regardless of my example, you will have to consider the situation and decide if you wish to add the company with a lower dividend growth rate to your list.

2. **A company has not met the 5% dividend growth rule for the past five years.**
   If a company has posted 10% or higher dividend growth for several years then suddenly that growth drops below 5%, this may be an indication that the company's earnings has slowed and therefore the dividend growth will slow. When you see a significant drop, for example from 10% to 3% or 2%, then to me, this is a clear sign the company is just paying a minimum dividend increase to maintain their aristocrat status.
   But there are companies where the dividend growth is normally at a lower rate, for instance below 10% that periodically falls below 5%. I suggest you may not

want to eliminate some of these firms from your selection, after looking into their past history and future prospects.

3. **A company you are interested in, is not on the Dividend Aristocrat list.**
   There are good companies, many which pay and raise their dividend but do not have a 25 year history of doing so, which should not be over-looked. Should you find one and wish to consider it, apply the following six-step rules,:
   1. Eliminate the company if they have cut their dividend in the past 10 years.
   2. Has the company paid a dividend for a minimum of 10 years?
   3. Has the company had a consistent record of raising their dividend for 10 years (The more often the increase, the better the stock)?
   4. Has the dividend grown over the past 10 years by at least 95%?
   5. Has the dividend growth for the past five years been 5% or more per year?
   6. Is the current yield of the stock above 1%?

*Note: I am providing these "exception rules" as I don't want you to overlook a good company just because it currently does not meet all my guidelines. Still, each stock should be assessed individually, in the end, it is up to you to determine your comfort level in eliminating them or not.

NOTICE: Morningstar changed their Home screens and method of accessing the dividend data we which to find. You do need to Sign Up and just use the Free Access.

Once you've registered and Logged-In, you will be able to access the data by following steps listed in the next section.

I will also mention other sources and the procedures to get the data we seek from those sources as well.

Using Value Line:

If you can access Value Line online through your library, then you'll be able to obtain most of the information you need easily and all in one place. Here is where to find the data:

1. Enter company Symbol
2. Click on PDF Reports, and current listing
3. You'll see the Div'ds per share, and the Ave yields
4. Plus other data on the company

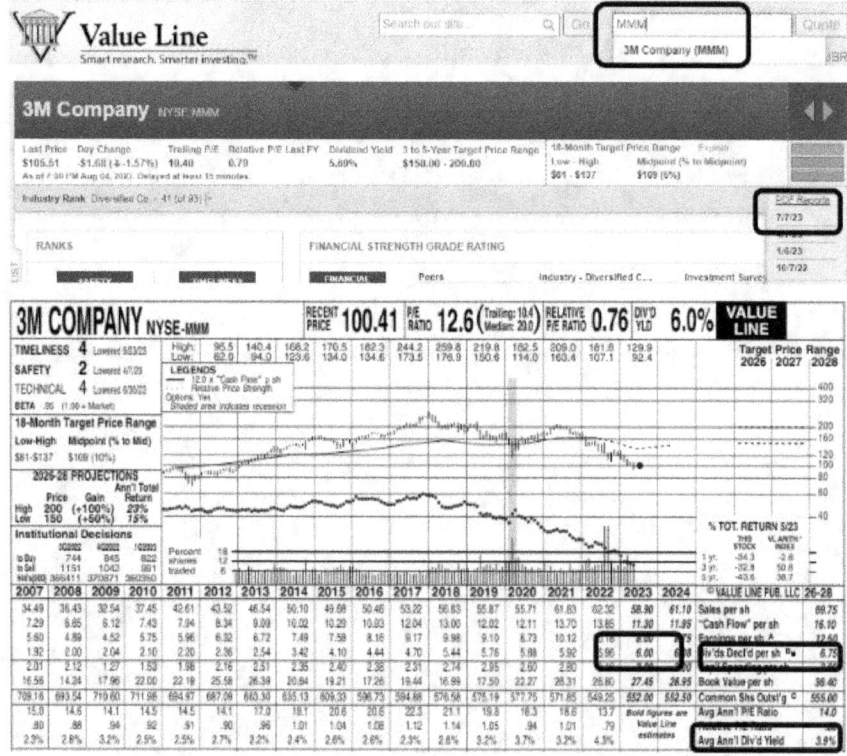

The information you'll need is circled.

How to apply the three rules: Using Morningstar.

Login into the Morningstar website:
https://members.morningstar.ca/login.aspx#334-hidenews

Enter the stock symbol, I'll use ABBV for AbbVie Inc.

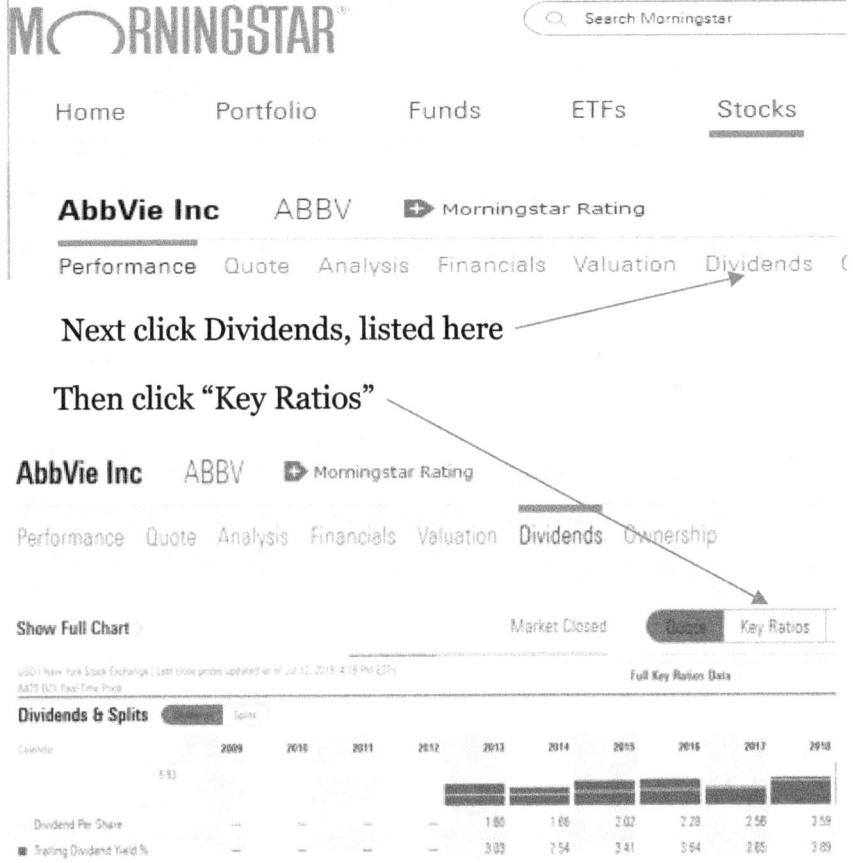

You will see the screen above showing the Dividends Per Share and Trailing Dividend Yield % for each year.

There is a scroll bar ab the bottom to move the screen to the right to see later figures. You can next click Full Key Ratios Data at the top of the data.

AbbVie Inc ABBV | ★★★★

Financials

Export 📄 | Ascending

	2009-12	2010-12	2011-12	2012-12	2013-12	2014-12	2015-12	2016-12	2017-12	2018-12
Revenue USD Mil	14,214	15,638	17,444	18,380	18,790	19,960	22,859	25,638	28,216	32,753
Gross Margin %	71.5	72.5	73.4	75.5	75.6	77.8	80.3	77.2	75.0	76.4
Operating Income USD Mil	5,102	4,717	4,293	5,817	5,664	3,411	7,537	9,384	9,592	6,383
Operating Margin %	35.9	30.2	24.6	31.6	30.1	17.1	33.0	36.6	34.0	19.5
Net Income USD Mil	4,637	4,178	3,433	5,275	4,128	1,774	5,144	5,953	5,309	5,687
Earnings Per Share USD	—	—	—	3.35	2.56	1.10	3.13	3.63	3.30	3.66
Dividends USD	—	—	—	—	1.60	1.66	2.02	2.28	2.56	3.59
Payout Ratio % *	—	—	—	—	42.0	71.3	112.9	60.0	60.4	67.8
Shares Mil	1,580	1,580	1,580	1,577	1,604	1,610	1,637	1,631	1,603	1,546
Book Value Per Share * USD	—	—	—	2.13	2.25	2.92	3.02	4.06	4.20	-1.98
Operating Cash Flow USD Mil	5,367	4,976	6,247	6,345	6,267	3,549	7,535	7,041	9,960	13,427
Cap Spending USD Mil	-313	-448	-356	-333	-491	-612	-532	-479	-529	-638
Free Cash Flow USD Mil	5,055	4,528	5,891	6,012	5,776	2,937	7,003	6,562	9,431	12,789
Free Cash Flow Per Share * USD	—	—	—	3.81	3.47	2.96	2.73	4.25	5.26	7.58
Working Capital USD Mil	—	4,457	1,457	8,578	10,969	4,688	5,420	6,406	4,582	-294

Review the dividends paid each year.

1. ABBV has only paid a dividend since 2013, this makes you wonder why this stock is listed as a Dividend Aristocrat. Possibly because it is a spinoff of Abbott Laboratories (ABT), but with only five or six years of dividend payments we could eliminate this stock.

Earnings Per Share USD	3.12	3.69	2.96	3.01	3.72	1.62	1.49	2.92	0.94	0.27
Dividends USD	1.41	1.56	1.72	1.88	2.01	0.56	0.88	0.96	1.04	1.06
Payout Ratio % *	—	42.3	58.1	63.4	54.0	22.3	63.5	56.3	154.6	87.9

Symbol	Company	Payout Ratio	Symbol /Yield	2008	2009	2010	2011	2012	2013	2014	2015	2016	2017	2018
ABBV	AbbVie Inc.	54.27	ABBV						1.6	1.66	2.02	2.28	2.56	60.00%
			4.92%											
ABT	Abbott Laboratories	44.57	ABT	0.705	0.78	0.86	0.94	1.005	0.56	0.88	0.96	1.04	1.06	50.35%
			1.60%		10.64%	10.26%	9.30%	6.91%	-44.28%	57.14%	9.09%	8.33%	1.92%	

For the next example, let's look up ABT.

2. ABT's dividends split in 2013 (2.0842 shares for one share, just over a 2-1 split), so the 10 year dividends are .68, .75, .83, .90, .96, **.56**, .88, .96, 1.04, 1.06.

Because of the ABBV spinoff the dividend seems to be cut, but owners of ABT would have received ABBV shares. Record the dividends on the worksheet: The dividend growth for ABT is only 50.35% so it would not make your List of Stocks to Consider. Depending upon the ABBV shares you received, you may yet want to add it.

3. Now let's check ADM's dividend history, following the procedure we used for ABBV.

Earnings Per Share USD	2.79	2.62	3.00	3.13	1.84	2.02	3.43	2.98	2.16	2.79
Dividends USD	0.49	0.54	0.58	0.62	0.69	0.76	0.96	1.12	1.20	1.28
Payout Ratio % *	–	–	–	–	–	48.6	31.3	37.5	45.0	59.2

We see that they have paid and raised the dividend each year. Let's check the dividend growth rate by recording the beginning and ending dividend in our spreadsheet over the 10 years and calculate the percentage growth. Record the beginning dividend, 0.49. It ended up at 1.28 in 2017, so (1.28-0.49)/0.49 x 100 = 161%. This shows a percentage above the 95% dividend growth rate, the dividend growth is above 5% the past five years (see chart below) and yield is above 1%, so ADM passes all three-rule tests and should be added to your "**List of Stocks to Consider**".

Continue to check the Dividend Aristocrat stocks and record your findings on the listing sheet. Though we eliminated ABBV and ABT, I suggest you enter their data in all the columns, calculating the year-to-year percentage growth and 10-year dividend growth rate.

I recommend that you keep data for all stocks you analyze, even adding extra comments and impressions, regardless of purchase. It is very useful to track stock performance of all companies, it usually confirms, with a quick glance, why you would purchase, or not, any stock. I have provided a few more examples of how I applied the three-rule tests with ADP, AFL, AOS, APD & BDX on the chart below, this should give you a good idea of how the Excel spreadsheet works within the process.

Sym	Payout Ratio	Symbol /Yield	2008	2009	2010	2011	2012	2013	2014	2015	2016	2017	2018	Comments
ABBV	54.27	ABBV						1.6	1.66	2.02	2.28	2.56	60.00%	No, only 5yrs
		4.92%												
ABT	44.57	ABT	0.705	0.78	0.86	0.94	1.005	0.56	0.88	0.96	1.04	1.06	50.35%	No, slow growth
		1.60%		10.64%	10.26%	9.30%	6.91%	-44.28%	57.14%	9.09%	8.33%	1.92%		
ADM	38.75	ADM	0.49	0.54	0.58	0.62	0.69	0.76	0.96	1.12	1.2	1.28	161.22%	Yes, good growth
		2.99%		10.20%	7.41%	6.90%	11.29%	10.14%	26.32%	16.67%	7.14%	6.67%		
ADP	73.08	ADP	1.28	1.35	1.42	1.54	1.7	1.88	1.95	2.08	2.24	2.52	96.88%	Possible exception
		1.98%		5.47%	5.19%	8.45%	10.39%	10.59%	3.72%	6.67%	7.69%	12.50%		
AFL	26.28	AFL	0.48	0.56	0.57	0.61	0.67	0.71	0.75	0.79	0.83	0.87	81.25%	No, slow growth
		2.17%		16.67%	1.79%	7.02%	9.84%	5.97%	5.63%	5.33%	5.06%	4.82%		
AOS	33.65	AOS	0.12	0.13	0.14	0.15	0.18	0.23	0.3	0.38	0.48	0.56	366.67%	Yes, good growth
		1.66%		8.33%	7.69%	7.14%	20.00%	27.78%	30.43%	26.67%	26.32%	16.67%		
APD	61.86	APD	1.79	1.92	2.23	2.50	2.77	3.02	3.20	3.39	3.71	4.25	137.43%	Yes, good growth
		2.65%		7.26%	16.15%	12.11%	10.80%	9.03%	5.96%	5.94%	9.44%	14.56%		
BDX	28.22	BDX	1.32	1.48	1.64	1.80	1.98	2.18	2.40	2.64	2.92	3.00	127.27%	No, under 5%
		1.22%		12.12%	10.81%	9.76%	10.00%	10.10%	10.09%	10.00%	10.61%	2.74%		
BEN	32.95	BEN	0.28	0.29	0.33	0.36	0.39	0.48	0.60	0.72	0.80	0.92	228.57%	

This exercise is important because this book is not intended to provide you with a list of recommended stocks to choose from. I would rather provide you with the tools, a process by which to gather and analyze the data, so that you can make your own decisions. Once you become comfortable with this method of evaluation, you can apply it to any stock, or any index.

I have liken my three-rule test to a "Dividend Growth Sluice", to separate out the cyclical, low-quality and low growth stocks, to be left with those few gems, the dividend growth payers!

Calculating 10 Year Average Yields

For just the stocks that you feel pass the Four-Rule test, I now suggest you calculate the 10 year average yield percentages. Morningstar only provided 5 years of Trailing Yield percentages, so to calculate the 10 year Average yield for any of the stocks, I'll obtain the information from Yahoo Finance.

You need to record the 10 year dividends paid from Morningstar onto the "%Gth Yld" Excel worksheet.

	2009	2010	2011	2012	2013	2014	2015	2016	2017	2018	Gth/Yld Ave
Dividend											#DIV/0!
% Chg		#DIV/0!	#DIV/0!	#DIV/0!	#DIV/0!	#DIV/0!	#DIV/0!	#DIV/0!	#DIV/0!	#DIV/0!	
Price											
Yield	#DIV/0!	#DIV/0!	#DIV/0!	#DIV/0!	#DIV/0!	#DIV/0!	#DIV/0!	#DIV/0!	#DIV/0!	#DIV/0!	#DIV/0!

	2009	2010	2011	2012	2013	2014	2015	2016	2017	2018	Gth/Yld Ave
Dividend											#DIV/0!
% Chg		#DIV/0!	#DIV/0!	#DIV/0!	#DIV/0!	#DIV/0!	#DIV/0!	#DIV/0!	#DIV/0!	#DIV/0!	
Price											
Yield	#DIV/0!	#DIV/0!	#DIV/0!	#DIV/0!	#DIV/0!	#DIV/0!	#DIV/0!	#DIV/0!	#DIV/0!	#DIV/0!	#DIV/0!

For this sample I'll use ADM. We will have already gotten the dividend paid each year from Morningstar, so we need only obtain the price to use at the end of each year. Actually I'm going to use the price just after the dividend was paid.

Let's go to the Yahoo website:

https://ca.finance.yahoo.com/quote/%5EGSPTSE/history/

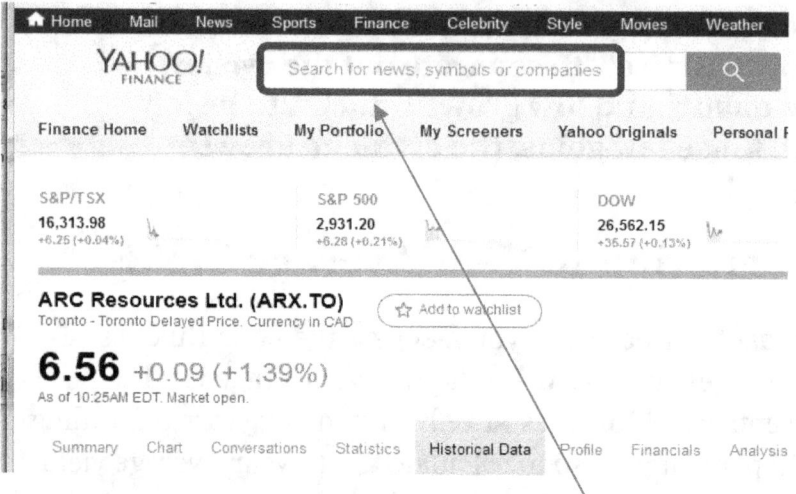

1. Enter the Symbol, in this case ADM and search
2. Click Historical Data
3. Click the Dates by the Time Period and enter they beginning year you wish, I'm using 1/01/2009:

4. Change the Frequency to **"Monthly"**, then click **"Apply"**

5. Arrow down to the last dividend paid in 2009

Jan. 01, 2010	31.48	31.89	29.52	29.97
Dec. 01, 2009	31.25	31.98	29.91	31.31
Nov. 17, 2009				0.14 Dividend

6. Record the price shown just above the dividend (the fourth number) or $31.31 and record the figure on the "%Gth Yld" Price cell for 2009.

ADM	2009	2010	2011	2012	2013	2014	2015	2016	2017	2018	Gth/Yld Ave
Dividend	0.54	0.58	0.62	0.69	0.76	0.96	1.12	1.20	1.28	1.34	148.15%
% Chg		7.41%	6.90%	11.29%	10.14%	26.32%	16.67%	7.14%	6.67%	4.69%	
Price	31.31										
Yield	1.72%	#DIV/0!	#DIV/0!	#DIV/0!	#DIV/0!	#DIV/0!	#DIV/0!	#DIV/0!	#DIV/0!	#DIV/0!	#DIV/0!

7. Arrow up to find the last dividend paid for 2010 and record the price, in the fourth column, on your worksheet. Continue to record each year closing price.

8. When finished the yearly yields will be shown and the Averge Yield for the 10 years, in this case 2.41%, as will the dividend growth for the 10 years, 148.15%.

ADM	2009	2010	2011	2012	2013	2014	2015	2016	2017	2018	Gth/Yld Ave
Dividend	0.54	0.58	0.62	0.69	0.76	0.96	1.12	1.20	1.28	1.34	148.15%
% Chg		7.41%	6.90%	11.29%	10.14%	26.32%	16.67%	7.14%	6.67%	4.69%	
Price	31.31	30.08	28.60	27.39	43.40	52.00	36.68	45.65	40.08	40.97	
Yield	1.72%	1.93%	2.17%	2.52%	1.75%	1.85%	3.05%	2.63%	3.19%	3.27%	2.41%

9. Follow the same process, using the Morningstar dividend data and Yahoo price data to calculate the Dividend Growth % and the Average Yield % for stock you wish. There are plenty of company blank data on the "%Gth Yld" worksheet.

10. *Remember to save the worksheet. I suggest you use "Save As" giving the worksheet a new name, such as 2019 Stock Analysis or 2019 My Stock Worksheet. Every time you update or change the data re-save immediately.

2ⁿᵈ. Data Source, Using the Dividend Channel.

This method requires a better knowledge of Excel, but I'll try to provide a step-by-step explanation.

Go to The Dividend Channel online:

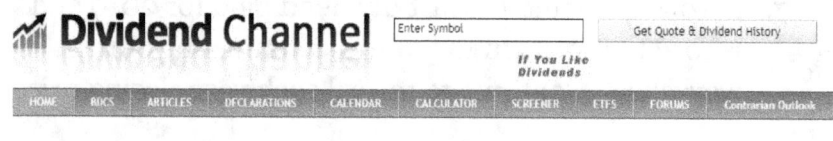

https://www.div*idendchannel.com/history/

In the box "Enter Symbol" type the company symbol.

Type in the company symbol you wish to evaluate in the box Fund/Stock at the top that you wish to research. I'll use ABT, Abbott Laboratories as my example.

Dividend Channel `ABT`

Arrow down till you see the Dividend History on the right side:

DIVIDEND HISTORY

Date	Div*
04/12/19	0.320
01/14/19	0.320
10/12/18	0.280
07/12/18	0.280
04/12/18	0.280
01/11/18	0.280
10/12/17	0.265
07/12/17	0.265

*Here's where the tricky part comes in for some:

You will need to download my Sample Excel worksheets from:

https://drive.google.com/drive/u/1/folders/1kD-ZtK7WkIINobzB3HYJ1tnwnh9P3NDf

Open up the 70 Qtr Div or 20 Mo Div tab (depending whether the dividend is paid Quarterly or Monthly.

Quarterly Dividends		Monthly Dividends	
12/13/2018	0.755	12/28/2018	0.05
9/13/2018	0.755	11/29/2018	0.05
6/14/2018	0.755	10/30/2018	0.05
3/14/2018	0.755	9/27/2018	0.05
12/14/2017	0.718	8/30/2018	0.05
70 Qtr Div	20 Mo Div	70 Qtr Div	20 Mo Div

We want to copy 10 years of Dividend History and insert the data into the Excel worksheet. The samples above show that both worksheets look the same, but notice the dates of the dividend payments, one is quarterly the other monthly.

To copy the dividends from the Dividend Channel:

1. Find the latest full year dividends, in this case it's 2019, so we start with Nov 20, 2019 for ADM
2. Left Click, and Hold the left mouse button down on the 11/20/2019 and

Date	Div*
11/20/19	0.350
08/21/19	0.350
05/14/19	0.350
02/15/19	0.350
11/21/18	0.335
08/15/18	0.335

DIVIDEND HISTORY

3. Drag the mouse down to the dividend paid for 10 years, which will be the first 2009 payment (01/13/09 for ABT)
4. If you go past the Jan 2009 date, move the mouse back up, not releasing the Left mouse button
5. When you have the 01/13/09 date and dividend paid highlighted release the Left mouse button. ***If you don't get the section highlighted you will have to try again.**

11/15/11	0.175
08/16/11	0.160
05/17/11	0.160
02/15/11	0.160
11/16/10	0.150
08/17/10	0.150
05/18/10	0.150
02/16/10	0.150
11/17/09	0.140

6. To copy the highlighted data, Hold the "Ctrl" button down and press the letter "C". Ctrl C is copy.
7. Go to the Excel worksheet and open the 70 Mo Div. worksheet as ADMs dividend is quarterly
8. Click on the cell to the right of Copy Data > and below Quarterly Dividends.

Monthly Dividends

Copy Data > [   ]

9. Hold the "Ctrl" key and press "V". Ctrl V is to paste.

Quarterly Dividends

Copy Data >	11/20/2019	0.35	
	8/21/2019	0.35	
	5/14/2019	0.35	
	2/15/2019	0.35	1.40
	11/21/2018	0.335	
	8/15/2018	0.335	
	5/16/2018	0.335	
	2/16/2018	0.335	1.34
	11/15/2017	0.32	
	8/15/2017	0.32	
	5/16/2017	0.32	
	2/16/2017	0.32	1.28

10. * This worksheet allow for 70 Quarterly companies (and 20 for Monthly Dividend companies) to be entered. Each is listed below the first, so you would arrow down to the next section for the next company paying a monthly dividend.

11. The data will be summarized above with the 10 yr. Div Gth calculated:

ADM	2010	2011	2012	2013	2014	2015	2016	2017	2018	2019	10 Yr Gth%
Dividend	0.58	0.62	0.69	0.76	0.96	1.12	1.20	1.28	1.34	1.40	141.38%
Div Gth Yr		6.90%	11.29%	10.14%	26.32%	16.67%	7.14%	6.67%	4.69%	4.48%	
Price											10yr Ave Yld
Yield %	####	####	####	####	####	####	####	####	####	####	#DIV/0!
Current Yld	####										

Now we want to obtain the Stock Price at the end of each year in order to determine the Year to Year change in the Dividend Yield.

To obtain this information I will use Yahoo Finance. https://ca.finance.yahoo.com/quote/%5EGSPTSE/history/

Follow the same process described earlier.

11. When finished the year-to-year yields will be shown and the 10 year average yield.

ADM	2009	2010	2011	2012	2013	2014	2015	2016	2017	2018	Gth/Yld Ave
Dividend	0.54	0.58	0.62	0.69	0.76	0.96	1.12	1.20	1.28	1.34	148.15%
% Chg		7.41%	6.90%	11.29%	10.14%	26.32%	16.67%	7.14%	6.67%	4.69%	
Price	31.31	30.08	28.60	27.39	43.40	52.00	36.68	45.65	40.08	40.97	
Yield	1.72%	1.93%	2.17%	2.52%	1.75%	1.85%	3.05%	2.63%	3.19%	3.27%	2.41%

12. At the right add your opinion if you feel the company should be added to your List of Stocks to Consider.

J	K	L	M	N
12-Oct-16	12-Oct-17	12-Oct-18	10 Yr Gth%	Consider Y/N
1.04	1.06	1.12	49.53%	No, low Growth
8.33%	1.92%	5.66%		
38.07	56.37	74.05	10yr Ave Yld	
2.73%	1.88%	1.51%	2.48%	

13. Repeat the above process for each stock you are researching, recording them in the appropriate sheet.

14. Also record your findings on the Stock Summary

	26 Dividend Aristocrats List of Stocks to Consider		
1	ARCHER DANIELS MIDLAND CO	ADM	Consumer
2			Consumer
3			Consumer
4			Consumer
5			Consumer

worksheet and record your comments.

15. *Remember to save the worksheet. I suggest you use "Save As" giving the worksheet a new name, such as 2019 Stock Analysis or 2019 My Stock Worksheet. Every time you update or change the data re-save immediately.

When you have finished your analysis, you may wish to compare your results to mine.

When you have finished your analysis, compare your results to mine.

I eliminated 28 Aristocrats initially, but after applying the subsequent exception rules, I added 2 back in, resulting in a final tally of 26 cut and 31 quality stocks out of 57 for my, "List of Stocks to Consider".

There is no right or wrong answer on how many you eliminate or keep. I think less is better if you are just starting your income investment journey. I want to keep things simple by sticking with the best DG stocks you can find. You do not have to buy or even consider buying all the stocks on your list, you are just complying a list of stocks to choose from, when they are reasonably priced (which is discussed later). When it comes to purchasing stocks, it will be much easier to choose from 15 to 31 than 57.

As I mentioned before there will always be exceptions on whether to add a stock or not. Consider each on their unique merits. I'd rather you feel you've selected the best, not the most. I hope you, like me, will be attracted to the "Steady Eddies": the stocks with a long history of sharing their earnings, these stocks increase their payout to shareholders each year.

I'll talk more about dividend growth later, but if you find a company that increases their dividend each year, even if it's only by as little as 5%, remember that it is this percentage increase that will build your future wealth. The growth may begin slowly, but the longer you hold the stocks and the more funds you add over time, the faster your income will grow.

We are not looking for short-term quick growth, but long-term sustained growth.

Personal Note: The three-rule (or six-rule for other stocks) test is much more important than it may seem at first glance. It almost seems too simple to believe that it actually works, but I can confirm that it really does. Use it every chance you get to analyze any stock or stocks within a fund. I think you'll come to the same conclusion I have, that the three-rule test is an easy and quick way to determine if a company is a quality income (dividend) stock. That's our main focus, finding stocks that will generate the income you seek.

By performing the three-rule test on the Dividend Aristocrats stocks, you might be satisfied with the list as is, but there are a few more things you might wish to examine before making your final selection. The following section will concentrate on this next level of analysis:

Check a company's long-term dividend history chart:

To check the "Long-Term Dividend Charts" of companies, go to The Dividend Channel online:

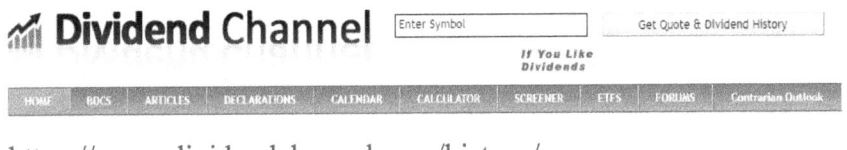

https://www.dividendchannel.com/history/

Again, we are checking stocks on the Dividend Aristocrats, and I will use Abbott Laboratories (ABT) as an example. You may not wish to check all the stocks you have eliminated, but you should check a few just to confirm your initial findings.

Enter the company symbol "ABT", and review the chart illustrating its dividend history (I have provided a screenshot 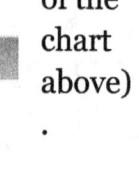 of the chart above).

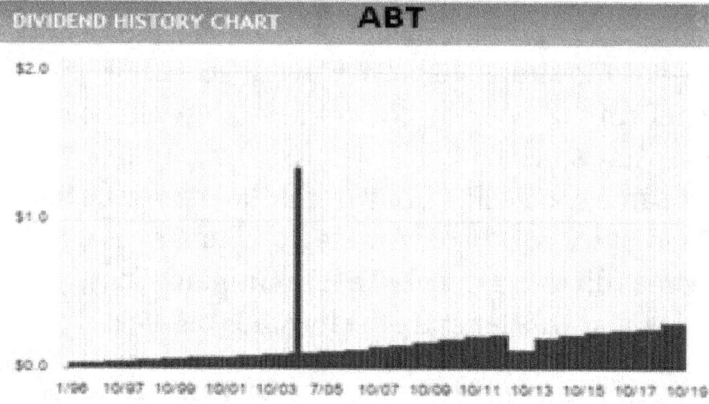

If you remember, I eliminated ABT using the three-rule test, for its low dividend growth, and after looking at its 20-year dividend chart, it seems to confirm my initial decision. This demonstrates the importance of dividend growth in choosing quality stocks. It also helps to see a company's growth pattern in a visual form, I find these charts very useful as an "at a glance" reference.

Now let's look at ADM's dividend growth history.

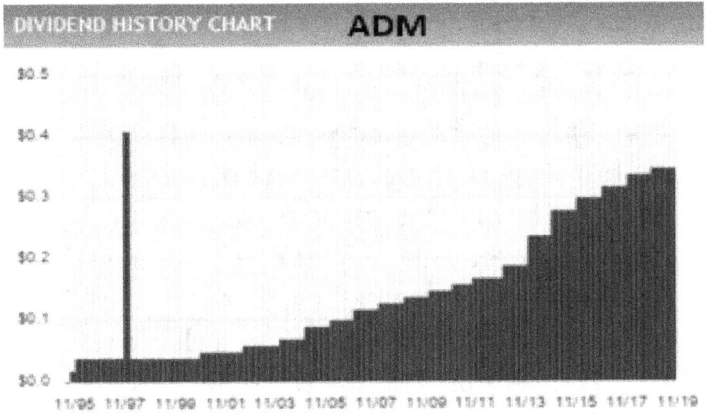

ADM is an example of a three-rule "yes" stock on my list. ADM shows a good dividend growth chart, despite a flat period between 1996 and 2000, and a steady dividend increase after that.

I want to provide two other examples with CVX and JNJ. CVX has had a long history of solid dividend growth, but its growth began to slow, falling below 5% in 2015 and continuing to drop. Looking at its dividend chart, below, you will see how it confirms why I did not be add it to my List of

	2008	2009	2010	2011	2012	2013	2014	2015	2016	2017	10yr Gth
Chevron	2.53	2.66	2.84	3.09	3.51	3.90	4.21	4.28	4.29	4.32	70.75%
		5.14%	6.77%	8.80%	13.59%	11.11%	7.95%	1.66%	0.23%	0.70%	

Stocks to Consider. The dividend growth has gone way down for the past three years.

Now we will look at JNJs chart: Even with only a 85.47% 10-year dividend growth rate, JNJ is one I added back to my list of stocks to consider. Just a quick glance at its dividend growth chart can help explain why!

	2008	2009	2010	2011	2012	2013	2014	2015	2016	2017	10yr Gth
JNJ	1.80	1.93	2.11	2.25	2.40	2.59	2.76	2.95	3.15	3.32	84.44%
		7.22%	9.33%	6.64%	6.67%	7.92%	6.56%	6.88%	6.78%	5.40%	

The JNJs long-term dividend chart is ideal, a steady and continuous increase over time. Truly a "Steady Eddie".

I recommend applying the three-rule test to the stocks before looking at their 20-year dividend chart. As much as I like to recommend reviewing charts, sometimes they can be deceiving, depending upon how they are presented and the number spread used on the chart. The three-rule test and 10-year analysis provides a clearer picture of a company's current status. Use the Dividend Channel charts to view a longer time period, especially for those stocks you might have listed as "exceptions", or when you might want to take another look at a stock that didn't initially make your list.

Note:* At this point and going forward, using Excel is very important. My stock analysis relies heavily on being able to track changes in yield and dividend growth, to calculate percentages and averages. I know not everyone is familiar or comfortable with this program, and I apologise for referring to it so frequently, however, I cannot recommend enough that you find a way to incorporate Excel (or a similar spreadsheet program) in your investment tracking should you wish to adopt my income growth strategy.

Review a company's year-to-year dividend yield percentage change:

This is the percentage change of the dividend from one year to the next.

We already performed this calculation as part of the three-rule test, but it so important that I felt it was worth emphasizing here.

It is important to note that the year-to-year change in dividend growth is probably more important than the long-term average, especially if the dividend growth percentage is dropping. I prefer to see a consistent growth percentage, one that does not vary too much from year to year.

When there is a sudden or extended drop in the dividend growth rate, especially if the increase drops below 5%, one should try to find out why. Have earnings dropped? Has the company made some large capital expenditure? Has there been a large loss or lawsuit? The question is, can the decrease be explained, and is it expected to continue or is it a short-term adjustment?

Low Yield, High Dividend growth: The lower the yield, the less current income, but if the dividend growth is at a higher rate, then over the long-term the dividend growth will likely drive the price of the stock higher.

With this step I want to demonstrate how a low dividend yield, with a high dividend growth record may be acceptable for long-term investors. Using Morningstar.ca, let's look at Cintas Corp's (CTAS) current yield. As of this writing, it is 1.09% which is lower than most of the past 10 years and its 10-year average of 1.36%. This indicates that the price has gone up and makes it slightly on the expensive side.

	2009	2010	2011	2012	2013	2014	2015	2016	2017	2018	10yr Ave
CTAS	1.80%	1.75%	1.55%	1.56%	1.29%	1.08%	1.15%	1.15%	1.04%	1.22%	1.36%
1.09%		-2.78%	-11.43%	0.65%	-17.31%	-16.28%	6.48%	0.00%	-9.57%	17.31%	

Next, let's pay attention to the 10-year average yield of CTAS, which is at 1.36% yield and year-to-year percentage change. Look at its dividend growth over the past 10 years which was

244.68%, going from 0.48 in 2008 to 1.62 in 2017 [(1.62-

CTAS	0.47	0.48	0.49	0.54	0.64	0.77	0.85	1.05	1.33	1.62	244.68%
1.09%		2.13%	2.08%	10.20%	18.52%	20.31%	10.39%	23.53%	26.67%	21.80%	

0.48)/0.48 x 100= 244.68%].

I can confirm that this is very good movement, and a reason to consider purchasing a stock with this kind of performance should the price drop in the future.

Why a good stock's yield is 1.5% to 3% above its average yield:

The higher yield above the 10-year average means the stock is cheaper and offers higher income than normal.

We will now investigate the reason why a stock meeting the basic three-rule test criteria has a dividend yield 2% to 3% above their 10-year average dividend yield. This is not an extremely high yield difference, but it should make one proceed with caution.

Exxon Mobil (XOM) is a good example of this situation. Morningstar shows, as of this writing, that XOM's current yield is 4.32%.

	2009	2010	2011	2012	2013	2014	2015	2016	2017	2018	10yr Ave
XOM	2.43%	2.38%	2.18%	2.52%	2.43%	2.92%	3.69%	3.30%	3.66%	4.74%	3.03%
4.32%		-2.06%	-8.40%	15.60%	-3.57%	20.16%	26.37%	-10.57%	10.91%	29.51%	

XOM's 10-year average dividend yield is 3.03%

This makes its current yield of 4.32%, higher than the average 10-year yield by 1.30%. Could this be considered a problem?

If you followed the news during this period, you'd know that there was concern about the drop in oil production and its fourth quarter came in below expectations. Management acknowledged the drop in oil production and refining margins and stated "the company is investing heavily to turn things around so it can grow earnings and cash flow in the coming years, including announcing a $50 billion bet on the U.S. energy sector". If that plan works, it could richly reward investors who choose to take advantage of the oil giant's recent sell-off. Regardless, one might feel XOM is still a solid stock, its dividend is safe and that this is an opportunity to buy its shares at a discounted price and increase one's income. If you find yourself comfortable with the decisions of management to deal with these challenges, then you could proceed to purchase. Remember, the decision is yours.

Consider a company's Payout Ratio:

Payout ratio is the portion of the company's annual earnings being paid out as dividends. To find a business's dividend-**payout ratio** for a given time period, use either the **formula** Dividends paid divided by Net income or Yearly dividends per share divided by Earnings per share. Those formulas are equivalent to each other.

Let's consider a company's Payout Ratio (see Definitions). For most companies 60% to 75% is a reasonable maximum, but utility companies usually go higher, around 80%. Because they often have long-term agreements and regulated prices, they can afford to pay more of their earnings out as dividends.

Now let's review the payout ratio for XOM. Return to Morningstar.ca and click on Key Stats. You can check the payout ratio history for any company at the same time as checking the dividend because payout ratio is listed just below the dividend.

Earnings Per Share USD	8.66	3.98	6.22	8.42	9.70	7.37	7.60	3.85	1.88	4.63
Dividends USD	1.55	1.66	1.74	1.85	2.18	2.46	2.70	2.88	2.98	3.06
Payout Ratio % *	—	41.7	27.9	21.9	22.5	31.3	33.2	59.9	138.3	99.0
Shares Mil	5,222	4,848	4,897	4,875	4,628	4,419	4,282	4,196	4,177	4,256
Book Value Per Share * USD	—	23.39	29.49	32.94	36.84	39.04	42.99	41.08	41.13	43.00
Operating Cash Flow USD Mil	59,725	28,438	48,413	55,345	56,170	44,914	45,116	30,344	22,082	30,066
Cap Spending USD Mil	-19,318	-22,491	-26,871	-30,975	-34,271	-33,669	-32,952	-26,490	-16,163	-15,402
Free Cash Flow USD Mil	40,407	5,947	21,542	24,370	21,899	11,245	12,164	3,854	5,919	14,664
Free Cash Flow Per Share * USD	—	1.23	4.40	5.59	4.73	2.83	3.57	0.98	0.16	3.61

The payout ratio for XOM has risen over a 10-year period, from 47.1% to 99.0% (paying more of its earnings as dividends). This is high, but the question is whether it's too high and will the company possibly cut its dividend. Earnings are shown to have dropped from 8.66 to 4.63, down 46.5%. It appears the dividend has increased faster than earnings and the high payout ratio is a concern. The one bright point is the jump in Free Cash Flow, more than doubling in the two previous years. This means the company does have cash available to support the dividend and it is not likely to be cut.

*The Free Cash Flow and Free Cash Flow per Share (see Definitions), can be seen lower down on the Key Stats screen. Free cash flow is the cash left over after a company pays for its operating expenses and capital expenditures.

I have not found another source for 10 year payout history, other than Morningstar. In Yahoo under "Statistics" you will see the current payout ratio of the stock listed. Compare the Payout Ratios for stocks in the same sector for a comparison. For example, you might compare the payout ratio of ADM to KO or PG and AOS to GD or 3M.

Avoid high yield stocks:

Stocks with a high dividend yield (in my opinion one above 7%) may have difficulty maintaining the dividend (may cut the amount) or not raise the dividend over time.

With the Dividend Aristocrats, only AT&T has a yield close to

	2009	2010	2011	2012	2013	2014	2015	2016	2017	2018	10yr Ave
T	5.85%	5.72%	5.69%	5.22%	5.12%	5.48%	5.46%	4.51%	5.04%	7.01%	5.51%
6.79%		-2.22%	-0.52%	-8.26%	-1.92%	7.03%	-0.36%	-17.40%	11.75%	39.09%	
										Above Ave Yld	1.28%

7%, currently 6.79%.

The current yield is 1.28% above its 10-year average yield, which is not excessively high.

When evaluating stocks other than the Dividend Aristocrats, I would look very carefully at any stock with a yield above 7%. It is more likely you will find that a high yielding stock will offer little or no dividend growth and likely little price growth and should be avoided.

Avoid cyclical stocks:

Finally, you should avoid cyclical stocks. Cyclical stocks are those affected by the ups and downs in the overall economy, such as airline, auto, technology, most energy, retail, consumer and mining stocks. When applying the three-rule test to the Dividend Aristocrats, you will most likely have found none are cyclical stocks, mainly because they normally cut their dividend when they are on a down cycle. Even if you are willing to take chances on stocks that do not fit my criteria, I recommend you avoid stocks that fall into the definition of cyclical.

Once you've put any of these considerations to practical use and seen how they affect any of the stocks on your **"List of Stocks to Consider"**, you may wish to add, remove or just make a note on any stocks for future reference.

Evaluation tools not considered:

It might be a good time to note that we have not looked at many of the other common stock evaluation methods, such as:

- Price to Earnings (P/E), Price to Sales and Price to Cash flow, Return on Equity.
- Estimating the intrinsic value of a stock, the discounted value of the cash that can be taken out of a business during its remaining life.
- Margin metrics, Gross Margin, Operating and Net.
- The Discounted Cash flow, future cash flows are estimated and discounted by using cost of capital to give their present values.

Most of these are used to determine if a stock is expensive, value priced, and/or to project its future earnings potential. Are they useful? Maybe, but they are more likely to be useful when one is seeking price growth from investments rather than income. This is also not a definitive list, there are as many ways to research and evaluate stocks as there are stock strategies to choose from.

Dividends are real and relevant markers, meaning the company either has the cash to pay the dividend or it does not. Reported earnings, on the other hand, may or may not be actual. I feel comfortable with the handful of steps I have provided and my experience with this method over the years.

The point I am trying to make is that my strategy is about simplification, but again I must stress that your comfort level is the priority, feel free to research as many forms of analysis as you wish.

I have narrowed a fairly large selection of companies to a few key dividend growth stocks using yield and dividend growth as our key evaluation measurement. I then applied even more tests for further consideration. It isn't a perfect test, but I do believe that by following the process I've outlined and by adding some common sense for good measure, you should feel comfortable with your results.

Your "**List of Stocks to Consider**" should now be complete, at least for the Dividend Aristocrat stocks (unless you wish to apply the six-rules to any other stock or fund). The next steps are:

- Group the stocks into sectors (banks, consumer, pipeline, telecom, utility, etc.).
- When you are ready to buy, choose the stocks, in the same sector, that are currently less expensive, or at least offering a better yield than the others.
- Remember, you do not have to own every stock on your list. You may start with a utility or telecom. Next you may buy a bank or pipeline and so on.
- Be aware that individual stocks and sectors will vary in price at different times.
- Once you've got a portfolio of 10 to 15 stocks in four or five sectors, you might wish to stick with those for a while, adding to them when the price or yield is attractive.
- If the market has a correction, you may be enticed to buy a particular stock which always seemed expensive but is now more reasonable.

I'd like to reiterate a point I will make often: I'd rather have a lot invested in a few good stocks, rather than the same amount (or more) in a group of mediocre stocks. Less is more.

With your list complete, ignore all other stocks that did not make your list!

Let's evaluate the NOBL ETF:

I mentioned earlier in my book that I do not recommend investing in ETFs (Exchange Traded Funds) for income, and it is only fair that I provide you with some specifics and hope you will come to the same conclusion.

NOBL is the ETF which holds the same 57 stocks as the Dividend Aristocrats. I used the Dividend Aristocrats as our source of companies to find qualifying stocks and applied the three-rule test to find our recommended dividend growth stocks. In my own analysis, I was able to eliminate 28 but added back two as exceptions, therefore eliminating 26 companies or 47.37% of the original 57, and I expect you will come close to the same number with your calculations.

By analyzing the NOBL ETF, we can see what it would be like to invest in all 57 stocks, rather than the best income providers of the group. Normally we ignore price, but for this comparison it will be meaningful to break this rule.

We will go to Morningstar.ca, find NOBL ETF, and then click on "Chart", then "10-years".

You will see that NOBL's price was $41.04 in Oct 2013 and a high of $68.30 in Sep. 2018, posting a 66.47% gain.

Feb 01, 2009 - Feb 01, 2019 • NOBL:23.13|56.76%

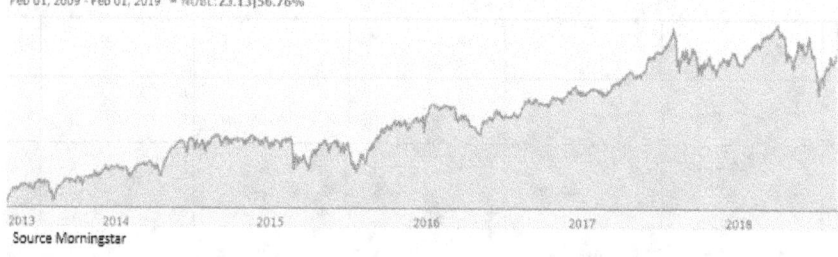

Source Morningstar

However, if I take a few of the companies from my own quality stock list, perhaps ADP (98.64% price growth), AOS

(155.19%), APD (74.54%) and ADM (36.11%), and review their 10-year charts for the same period, you will see that the average price growth for just those four is 91.12%.

You could continue to do the same check with other stocks on your list as I did, and like me, you will likely see that NOBL's performance will always be lower than the average of the stocks we will have separated from the whole. This is a very good example of how lower value stocks will drag down an ETF's overall performance, in my opinion, lessening the attraction and benefit of investing in any ETF.

To even further demonstrate my findings, go to The Dividend Channel website to check NOBLs 5-year distributions chart:

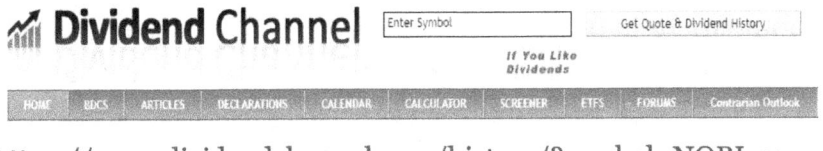

https://www.dividendchannel.com/history/?symbol=NOBL.ca

Enter "NOBL" where it says "Enter Symbol". Scroll down to see the 18-year Distribution chart:

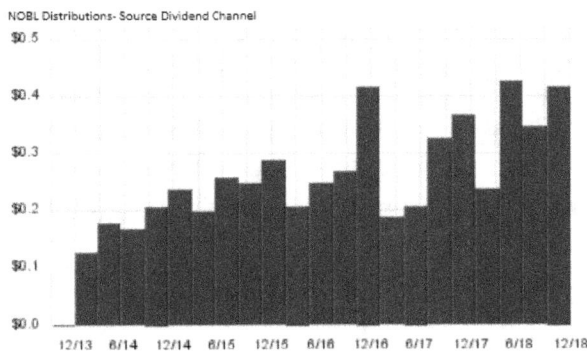

There are only five years of distributions, but they are erratic, going up and down, though dividend growth was 79.38% over the 5 years.

Compare NOBL with 5-year dividend charts (2013-2018) of

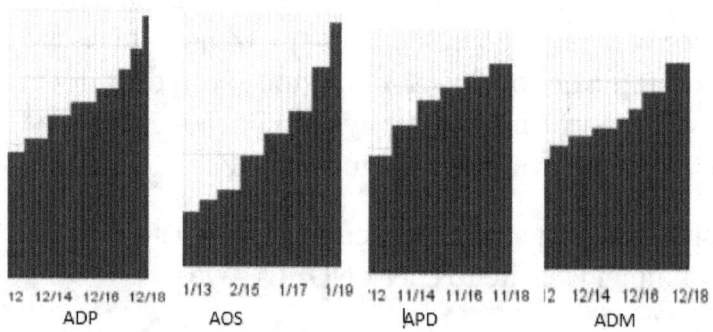

| 12 12/14 12/16 12/18 | 1/13   2/15   1/17   1/19 | 12 11/14 11/16 11/18 | 2   12/14 12/16 12/18 |
| ADP | AOS | APD | ADM |

ADP, AOS, APD and ADM:

When you compare the NOBL distribution chart to the charts of four stocks in my List of Stocks to Consider, NOBL comes out the loser. Feel free to check some of the other companies' dividend charts from your own list.

Further down, on the Dividend Channel you can see on the right 18 years of NOBL's quarterly distributions, from 2014 to 2018. I added up the quarterly distributions and entered 5 years, from 2013, on a yearly basis in an Excel spreadsheet.

NOBL Distributions

2018	2017	2016	2015	2014	Growth
1.435	1.114	1.15	0.995	0.8	79.38%
28.82%	-3.13%	15.58%	24.38%		

In 2017 the distribution **dropped by 3.13%** but for the 5 years the growth was 79.38%. This is less than our required 95% 10-year DG requirement from our three-rule test, but not too bad. However, the 10-year average dividend growth

70

of the 31 stocks on my list is **166.90%.** The 26 I eliminated only had an average 10-year dividend growth of 76.27%.

There is no guarantee that their dividend growth will continue at the high rate, but our analysis has attempted to select the best of the Dividend Aristocrats, giving us a better chance of obtaining our income goal. By selecting the entire 57 we would cut our chances in half.

I have provided the five top ETFs (out of 1,929) for 2018 in Appendix D for your review. Their distribution charts, price charts and the dividend growth percentages are shown to emphasize the points made in my analysis of NOBL.

Not many would recommend investing in a new stock (IPO) for income, because without an earnings and performance history it is considered speculative. Yes, there may be potential for substantial price gain, but few, if any, new offerings will become the next Apple, Facebook or Netflix. Yet when a new ETF is rolled out there seems to be a lot of excitement as they offer great diversification and low fees. That's the carrot, but where's the distribution and performance history? Not as speculative as an IPO but just as uncertain for future prospects, especially for an income investor.

If I haven't quite been able to convince you why, as an income investor, you should avoid ETFs, here is one more example I hope will do the trick. Vanguard is one of the country's largest ETF providers. They have added five new ETFs, created by combining several of their existing ETFs:

1. The Conservative Income ETF (VCIP) hold 80% bonds and 20% stocks,
2. The Conservative ETF (VCNS) holds 60% bonds and 40% stocks,

3. The Balanced ETF (VBAL) holds 60% stocks and 40% bonds,
4. The Aggressive ETF (VGRO) holds 80% stocks and 20% bonds.
5. The All-Equity ETF (VEQT) is 100% stocks.

On the outside, these "All-in One" ETFs would seem like there is something for everyone. Touted as total simplicity with low fees and no longer needing to worry about diversification, asset allocation and rebalancing. They take care of it all, but, I am simply not convinced of the benefits of these ETFs. Perhaps an analogy will help illustrate my point:

A man walks into a bar and asks for a glass of the best whiskey in the house, with water. The bartender carefully measures one ounce of his best spirit, then... abruptly pours it into a gallon of water and stirs! He nonchalantly pours out a glass, passes it to the man, and without a hint of irony says, "The first glass is on the house".

All five of the Vanguard funds have a whopping twelve thousand holdings each! Yes, I said 12,000. These funds must hold almost every stock and bond on the planet and trying to identify the best of their holdings might be akin to being able to taste the whiskey in that glass.

Chapter 4

Dividends are a wonderful gauge for management's confidence in forward looking profitability. (Paul Lim, New York Times, May 2, 2009)

What should the dividend yield be when buying?

I have mentioned checking a stock's current yield through the website Morningstar and comparing it to the stock's 10-year average yield to determine if the stock is reasonably priced or expensive. But how do you interpret this information and decide what yield makes a stock worth purchasing?

I feel that a high yield, above 7% and higher, is too high. These stocks will either be speculative (offering a high yield to entice investors), or stocks which may be experiencing financial difficulty (the perception of the stock is negative, driving down the price).

However, there are still a couple of choices to be made involving yields below 7%. Two possible scenarios to consider are the following:

1. A stock with a low dividend yield of 1.5% and less, but with a fairly high dividend growth rate of around 10% to 12% per year, or
2. A stock with an average dividend yield of 1.6% to 6.0% with an average dividend growth rate of around 5% to 8%.

I recommend that there is a place in one's portfolio for both, but my preference would be to hold a majority of stocks with a starting dividend yield of between 2.5% and 6%. Average-dividend yield stocks offer higher income from the start than low-yield stocks, and likely more sustainable dividend growth over time. This is especially true if the stock has a long history of growing the dividend at a reasonable rate, around 5% to 8%. For example, a stock with an initial dividend yield of 4% which grows its dividend 5% per year would have a yield of 7.92% after 15 years, which I feel is very reasonable. Low initial dividend yield around 0.62% and growth of 15% per year would result in a 4.4% dividend yield after 15 years. Not a great yield after 15 years, but price growth may be higher.

Stocks with a low yield and high dividend growth usually do offer higher capital appreciation (the price of their shares growing), provided they can continue to maintain their high dividend growth rate (usually 10% and above). We looked at CTAS earlier so let's check its stats:

CTAS, with a 2018 dividend yield of 1.06%, has had a dividend growth of 183.78% for the past 10 years.

Here is CTAS's dividend chart:

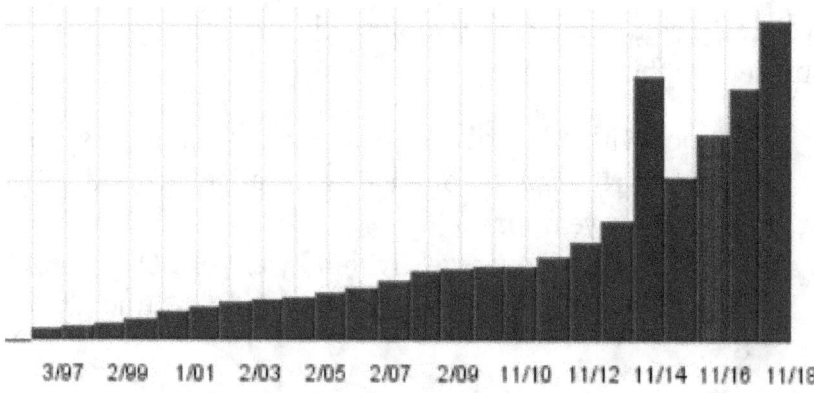

3/97 2/99 1/01 2/03 2/05 2/07 2/09 11/10 11/12 11/14 11/16 11/18

Now look at its price chart:

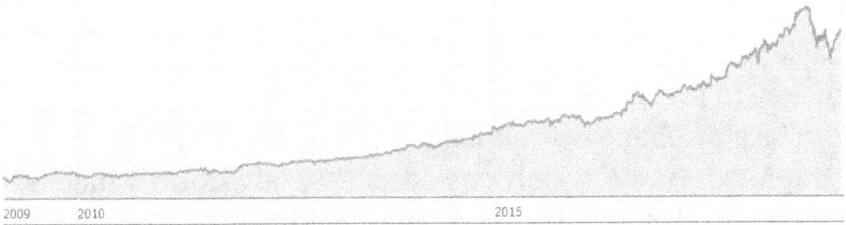

In 2009 the price was $23.98. At its peak on Sept. 2018 the price was $210.82, giving CTAS a 779.15% price growth.

In 2009 CTAS's yield was 1.80%, but if you had invested and held the stock, without making any further investments, your current yield on your investment would be 6.20%

We can't predict the future growth rate of each stock, but we do have support for our assumptions every time they pay and raise their dividend. If the low-yield, high-growth company can maintain its high growth rate, then the stock will offer a higher total return than the average-yield stocks in the long run.

Back to the question of what the starting yield should be. I don't recommend a particular starting yield, rather I suggest that when you are looking to buy a stock, based on your research, try to find stocks with a high yield in the sector of your choice. I do hesitate to buy, or recommend you buy, a stock with a yield less than 1%.

So, which stock to buy and when?

Once you have your list of stocks to consider, and you have money to invest, which stock should you buy and when? It can be a troubling decision, but one I believe can be simplified. How? By only considering to buy stocks which are currently offering you a reasonable yield.

In the previous section we discussed the difference between stocks which offer a low yield/high growth to average yield/average growth. I believe that you should own both, but you should only consider buying them when they offer a reasonable yield.

So, what is a reasonable yield? Well it varies for each stock, and you determine it by finding out what each stocks' long-term average yield is. This was explained under the section titled *"Calculating 10 Year Average Yields"* (page 45).

Once you know the 10-year average yield for each stock on your list of stocks to consider, then any stock which offers a higher yield than its long-term average yield is offering a reasonable yield. So, basically when you have money to invest, you compare the current yield of each stock to their 10-year average yield to determine the yield difference. For example:

SYMBOL	Current Price	Current Div	Current Yield	10 Yr Ave Yld	Yield Diff	Rating
MMM	$100.41	6.00	5.98%	3.90%	2.08%	Undervalued
ABT	$111.33	2.04	1.83%	1.60%	0.23%	Aveerage Priced
ADM	$82.83	1.80	2.17%	2.30%	-0.13%	Expensive
JNJ	$148.60	4.70	3.16%	2.50%	0.66%	Reasonably Priced

When you enter the current price for your stocks, the worksheet will calculate which stocks are Undervalued, Average Priced, Expensive, and Reasonably Priced.

Certainly, any stock which is Reasonably Priced should be considered a good stock to buy.

But when a stock is Undervalued, you should consider why there might be such a large yield difference. Has the company missed earnings estimate, has it a debt problem, or is it because of some economic factor? You must decide if the company is still viable, and if you consider the problem a short-term issue, then you have an opportunity to buy at low price.

You might consider Average Priced stocks, but you should avoid buying Expensive stocks.

Use the yield difference worksheet to help you decide which stocks might offer you a higher yield, above other stocks in the same sector.

Regardless whether the market is going up or down, there should always be a few stocks which offer a reasonable yield, and if every purchase made offers a higher yield than their long-term average, your long-term average yield will be higher.

How many stocks should you hold?

Seek quality individual stocks in a concentrated portfolio with low turnover (hold) and focus on the valuable far-flung future cash flow. (Tom Connolly, The Connolly Report)

How many stocks to hold in your portfolio(s) is a personal choice, there is no magic number. Some suggest 30, 50 or even 100 or more. The higher numbers are suggested in order that you hold sufficient stocks to be appropriately diversified (holding stocks in different sectors). Do not let others convince you to hold a large number of stocks across multiple sectors just to diversify. Again, you need to determine what your investment goals are, then build a portfolio accordingly.

However, if you are considering an income portfolio, I suggest starting with a lower number, I'll suggest 10 and then add only when you find a stock which meets your buy criteria. Don't just add stocks for diversification's sake, instead select stocks which will provide you with the income growth you are seeking. I've seen portfolios of 40 to 50 stocks and, in some cases, only a few dollars invested in each. That seems like a shotgun approach, especially when you are just starting out. Instead, I want you to identify those good "Steady Eddies" and buy as many shares as you can at a reasonable price. Kick-start your income growth-machine as quickly as possible.

You may still not be convinced that less is the way to go. Perhaps the following example will help persuade you (please excuse the Canadian stock I use as an example, as it supports the point I'm trying to express).

One day I read a very interesting headline;

"RBC executives may sell 30,000 shares." - IE
Investment Executive, July 6, 2005

Wow, I thought, how many shares do these RBC executives own? Probably more than most individual investors could ever accumulate. And why would they think of selling?

With this example, I want to show you the advantage of holding just one good DG stock, if the circumstances are to your advantage. In 2005, the Royal Bank dividend was $1.175 per share. If you only owned the Royal Bank stock, and held 30,000 shares in 2005, your annual income (dividends) would have been $35,250. Jump ahead to 2018 and you would now receive $114,000 per year of income (without reinvesting the dividends which would have increased the income considerably), a 223% increase in 14 years and an average of 9.64%/year.

Year	Shares	Div	Div Inc	Inc %
2005	30,000	1.18	$35,400	
2006	30,000	1.44	$43,200	22.03%
2007	30,000	1.82	$54,600	26.39%
2008	30,000	2.00	$60,000	9.89%
2009	30,000	2.00	$60,000	0.00%
2010	30,000	2.00	$60,000	0.00%
2011	30,000	2.08	$62,400	4.00%
2012	30,000	2.28	$68,400	9.62%
2013	30,000	2.53	$75,900	10.96%
2014	30,000	2.76	$82,800	9.09%
2015	30,000	3.04	$91,200	10.14%
2016	30,000	3.20	$96,000	5.26%
2017	30,000	3.48	$104,400	8.75%
2018	30,000	3.80	$114,000	9.20%
14 Years of Income			$1,008,300	9.64%

Better yet, look at the chart at left, and you will see that the income you would have received over the 14 years is **$1Million!**

If you were to apply the three-rule tests for Royal Bank and couple that with their long history of paying and growing their dividend, should lead you to the conclusion that it is likely that Royal Bank will continue as a good dividend growth stock.

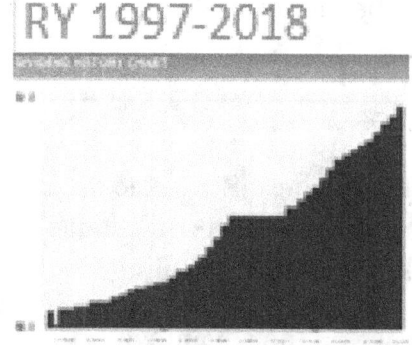

RY 1997-2018

Its dividend is most likely safe and will continue to grow as it has in the past. So, if you're fortunate enough to have 30,000 shares of a solid DG stock like Royal Bank, would you be concerned that you are not diversified? You would do better to hold on to it and take advantage of the growing income, rather than the one-time payoff of selling, or sell some of the shares to buy others just to diversify.

Owning 30,000 shares is a bit unrealistic for most investors, but what if you owned 300 shares in 2005? Let's look at the income you would have received over 14 years for these two

Royal Bank Div Fixed				Royal Bank Actual Div's			
Year	Shares	Div Rec	Inc Gth %	Year	Shares	Div Rec	Inc Gth %
2004	300.00			2004	300.00		
2005	315.92	$637.04		2005	316.78	$674.53	
2006	651.58	$667.45	4.77%	2006	657.44	$902.15	33.74%
2007	664.76	$682.77	2.30%	2007	679.53	$1,144.94	26.91%
2008	680.04	$696.86	2.06%	2008	709.81	$1,379.96	20.53%
2009	696.08	$714.56	2.54%	2009	742.25	$1,447.98	4.93%
2010	709.43	$729.01	2.02%	2010	769.81	$1,504.64	3.91%
2011	723.98	$742.99	1.92%	2011	801.11	$1,592.17	5.82%
2012	737.72	$758.38	2.07%	2012	833.79	$1,805.98	13.43%
2013	749.62	$772.02	1.80%	2013	865.84	$2,081.52	15.26%
2014	759.69	$783.69	1.51%	2014	896.91	$2,423.01	16.41%
2015	770.03	$794.02	1.32%	2015	932.96	$2,766.57	14.18%
2016	780.16	$805.04	1.39%	2016	971.09	$3,033.97	9.67%
2017	788.60	$814.68	1.20%	2017	1005.79	$3,345.88	10.28%
2018	796.85	$823.31	1.06%	2018	1043.53	$3,772.53	12.75%
Total Div Rec'd		**$9,784.77**	2.00%	**Total Div Rec'd**		**$27,201.31**	14.45%
				Income Difference		178.00%	

scenarios.

The chart on the left shows how much income you'd receive if the dividend stayed fixed at the 2005 rate. The right side is with the actual dividends paid (no dividend increases for 3 years, 2008-2010). Dividends are reinvested in both cases, so I feel confident stating that investing in a quality dividend growth stock is much more sound and profitable than a fixed income, CD or bond or low growth ETF.

I want to leave you with the idea that instead of worrying about how many stocks to own, concentrate on owning a smaller number of carefully selected stock picks. Stick to the list of stocks you compiled and avoid stocks that you haven't researched yourself and avoid buying ETFs which will dilute your total income. I am also not assigning a minimum number of stocks to hold, but rather recommend that you take advantage of buying opportunities of quality dividend growth (DG) stocks when the price drops. And, if you refer to the example of the Royal Bank from above, the more you have invested in fewer numbers of high performing dividend growth stocks, the better your income return will be. Remember, quality over quantity.

This is one of the foundations of my investing strategy and how I suggest you build an income-generating machine.

Personal Note: My wife and I at one time held between 35 and 40 stocks in all our accounts, but gradually eliminated most and now hold only 12 stocks in all of our accounts. We eliminated much of our portfolio because I continually reassessed our holdings and found some were not quality companies anymore, did not perform as well as we expected or had bought some stocks only for their higher yield. In hind sight we now know we would have been much better off with the concentrated portfolio right from the start. I hope to help you avoid my earlier missteps and start growing your income as soon as possible!

Those who cannot remember the past are condemned to repeat it. (George Santayana)

When does price matter?

If you are a saver and a buyer of shares–as most investors are and will continue to be for many years–your real long-term interest is, curiously, to have stock prices go down quite a lot and stay there so you can accumulate more shares at lower prices and therefore receive more dividends with the savings you invest. (Charles Ellis, Winning the Loser's Game)

....

For the stock you are considering to purchase, what we want is one with a good initial yield with a sustainable dividend growth. (Tom Connolly, The Connolly Report)

If you are investing small amounts of money, the price you pay for a stock should not be a concern (within reason). I want you to invest often and try to build up your holdings as quickly as possible. Let Dollar-Cost Averaging, which is buying more shares when the price is low and less when the price is high, even out the average cost of your investment.

For those investing larger amounts, try to buy when the price is low and/or your yield higher (a lower price means you will be buying more shares, and the higher yield means that you will be receiving more income). This does not mean waiting for the next market correction or trying to time the market, but, seeking reasonably priced stocks and knowing you are not paying a high price.

Here are a few simple methods to determine if the stock you wish to buy is value-priced (the price is low) and offers a good initial yield.

1. Compare the stocks' current yield (current annual dividend divided by the current price) against its 10-year average yield. I will use ADM and the Morningstar website to assist with our analysis. You can do this as well, go online to Morningstar and click the "Performance" tab and review the Dividend

History (04/02/2019)		2009	2010	2011	2012	2013	2014	2015	2016	2017	2018	
ADM		10.54	-2.01	-2.74	-1.78	61.23	22.03	-27.31	27.73	-9.40	5.56	
Farm Products			-2.19	20.40	-11.39	20.88	29.34	13.00	4.64	3.03	7.92	
+/- Farm Products			12.73	-22.42	8.65	-22.66	31.89	9.03	-31.95	24.69	-17.32	
Dividend Yield %		1.79	1.99	2.29	2.56	1.75	1.85	3.05	2.63	3.19	3.27	Ave Yld
Archer Daniels	ADM	1.79%	1.99%	2.29%	2.56%	1.75%	1.85%	3.05%	2.63%	3.19%	3.27%	2.44%
			11.17%	15.08%	11.79%	-31.64%	5.71%	64.86%	-13.77%	21.29%	2.51%	

Yield % line:

Here you will utilize your Excel spreadsheet again. Enter the yield percentages and calculate the Average Yield, in this case it works out to be 2.44%

You will see that ADM's current yield is 3.01% at Morningstar, showing that ADM is offering a higher yield than its average, which is good.

Another useful Excel worksheet I provide is the Yield Difference worksheet. Once you've determined the 10-year or long-term average yield for the stocks on your list, enter them into the Yield difference worksheet.

Then when you have money to invest, enter the current stock price for each stock, and the yield difference will be calculated, see the next chart:

SYMBOL	Current Price	Current Div	Current Yield	10 Yr Ave Yld	Yield Diff	Rating
MMM	$100.41	6.00	5.98%	3.90%	2.08%	Undervalued
ABT	$111.33	2.04	1.83%	1.60%	0.23%	Average Priced
ABBV	$138.64	5.92	4.27%	4.00%	0.27%	Average Priced
AFL	$69.43	1.68	2.42%	2.70%	-0.28%	Expensive
APD	$299.28	7.00	2.34%	2.10%	0.24%	Average Priced
JNJ	$148.30	4.45	3.00%	2.50%	0.50%	Reasonably Priced

The Rating column list the stocks as Undervalued, Average Priced, Expensive, and Reasonably Priced.

On should consider buying stocks, in the sector of your choice, when they are reasonably priced, or undervalued. Should an undervalued stock provide a 2% or higher yield difference, look into why there is such a large yield difference. Has the company missed its earning estimate, has some economic factor depressed prices for that sector, or has the company having some current financial difficulty.

Remember, that the stocks on your list are considered quality dividend growth stocks, and you believe that your investments in these companies are for the long-term. But even the best companies can have short-term difficulties, and though you may not wish to sell your shares, you may not add to your position, till you feel comfortable that the financial difficulties will not affect their long-term performance.

So, look to buy when the yield difference provides a reasonable difference, and take advantage of the undervalued stocks, when the market drops, and all of your stocks drop in value.

2. Another method is to compare the current price of the stock to the 52-week low price. *The Globe and Mail* provides a way to view daily updates of stock prices. Just go to their website, https://www.theglobeandmail.com/investing/mark

| Company | Symbol | As of February 4, 2019 | | | 52 Weeks | | Percentage Drop to Low Price | Percentage from High to Low $ |
		Latest Price	High	Low	High	Low		
Archer-Daniels	ADM	44.49	44.61	44.33	52.06	39.16	13.61%	32.94%
A.O.Smith	AOS	49.27	49.44	48.14	66.89	40.34	22.14%	65.82%
Air Products	APD	166.88	166.69	165.17	172.39	148.44	12.42%	16.13%

ets/portfolio/#/,

and set up a portfolio (you should be using the stocks you have chosen using the three-rule test). Concentrate on the 52-week high and the low prices.

The chart above shows that ADM is closer to the 52-week low (13.61%), than the high which agrees with the higher current yield than its 10-year average. Notice that APD is about in the middle between the high and low price.

3. For the third method, I recommend you set up an Excel worksheet to project what the dividend yield would be if the current price drops 3%, 5%, 8%, etc. If the stock price drops you can quickly see what yield you would receive, the chart I have provided shows the yield rises as the price decreases. The higher the

yield the more income you will receive for each dollar invested. That's a good thing!

Co.	Price Feb 4]19	Current Div	Current Yield	Ave 10 Yr Yld	3% Price Drop	Yield	8% Price Drop	Yield	10% Price	Yield
ADM	$44.49	$1.26	2.83%	2.44%	$43.16	2.92%	$40.93	3.08%	$40.04	3.15%
ADS	$49.27	$0.80	1.62%	1.24%	$47.79	1.67%	$45.33	1.76%	$44.34	1.80%
APD	$166.88	$4.33	2.59%	2.48%	$161.87	2.67%	$153.53	2.82%	$150.19	2.88%

4. The fourth method uses the Adjusted Cost Base (ACB) or the average cost of your stocks (if you already own stocks you will be familiar with this term). You can compare the current price of any stock you are considering buying to the ACB of the same stock you own. If the current price is close or lower than the ACB it may be a good time to buy.

5. Lastly, when you place your order with an online broker you can enter a "limit" price. This is the price you want to pay for the stock. The broker will not buy until the price reaches the price you set. You could intentionally enter a low price, of around 10% of the current price, leave the bid open for a month or so and wait to see if the order gets filled.

If a stock's yield is lower than its average (which indicates that the stock is expensive), don't feel you have to jump in immediately to buy. Stock prices can vary as much as 50%, though that's not the norm, over a 52-week period. If you don't get a stock at the price you want, don't worry as it's likely the price may drop later on. Be patient, or you can always keep researching for a more value-priced stock from your quality stock list.

We are not trying to buy at the lowest price possible (trying to time your purchases), but attempting to pay a reasonable price and ensure the purchases will contribute to our growing income. If you decided on a buy price, don't get upset if the price drops after you have bought. Continue to monitor the price and buy again when you have funds.

Reinvested Dividends:

Without dividend reinvestment, annual returns from stocks would be about as exciting as watching a silent movie. (Bill Staton, America's Finest Companies Investment Plan, 1989)

With dividend paying companies you have the choice of taking the money (leaving it in your broker account) or using the cash dividend to buy more shares. Most US brokers do offer full dividend reinvestment, which is the purchasing of fractions of shares, but you should still ask the question before opening the account. Also, with most brokers you must request or set up the account to automatically reinvest the dividends.

Every time you use your dividends to buy more shares you increase your next dividend payment. If you reinvest again you buy even more shares and the cycle repeats itself. Dividend reinvestment is one of the most important parts of my income investment strategy. If the broker does not offer Full Dividend reinvestment, then if you receive a $65.00 cash dividend and the current price of that share is $57.50 to buy only one share and $7.50 remains in the account. That's ok, if one is adding funds regularly to their account, the unused cash can be added to their next purchase. Many investors prefer to let the dividends accumulate in their account and combine them with new funds for their next purchase. Personally, I find this highly inefficient. What if you don't make the next purchase immediately or next month or even next quarter? Why not take advantage of commission-free reinvestment, even if only to ensure the regular accumulation of shares?

*Reinvesting dividends along with dividend growth is exactly what I mean by an ever-growing income!

The three keys to enhanced compounding are: buying quality dividend growth stocks, buying shares when they are value-priced and reinvesting the dividends.

That's what I mean by compounding, and I cannot emphasize enough its value as an income investment tool.

This subscribes to my philosophy of "hands-off" investing, by utilizing automatic reinvesting it takes a lot of work off your shoulders. You are in the process of constantly acquiring shares, if only a fraction of a share and those new shares will collect dividends and your dividends will become larger, and the cycle repeats. This is exactly what I mean by an ever-growing income!

For those just beginning, who invest only periodically, or are retired and no longer adding funds, you should accumulate fractions of shares, rather than only full shares.

To prove my point, I'd like you to look back to the example of my grandson (covered in Chapter 1). If I exclude the fractions of shares he was able to purchase, he would have only bought 60 full shares over the 11-year period. But he actually bought 80.9445 shares by being able to buy fractions of shares with his dividends. He received almost 21 additional shares or 33.33% more by simply utilizing dividend reinvestment.

That's a lot of extra shares that might not have been bought otherwise, a lot more income and very nice compounding, don't you agree?

How, where and what to invest:

> Think of stocks not only as providing a stream of income but actually as streams of income. You exchange your money for future cash flow. As the income grows with dividend increases, your original capital can grow too. An annuity, but better. (Josh Peters, founding editor of *Morningstar DividendInvestor*)

Dividend Reinvestment Plan (DRIP):

I don't want you to confuse Reinvesting Dividends, discussed in the previous section, with a Dividend Reinvestment Plan (DRIP). A DRIP is an investment plan offered directly by companies (usually through a Transfer Agent) and does not require one to open a brokerage account to buy shares or reinvest the dividends. DRIPs are ideally suited for those with limited funds to invest, perhaps less than $100 per month, or if you want to setup an investment for a minor (as with the example in Chapter 1). The advantages of investing by DRIPs are that one can invest small amounts commission free and the reinvested dividends purchase fractions of shares. (Full detail on how to setup DRIPs in detail see Appendix B).

* I am not fully familiar with US registered accounts, therefore the information on these pension accounts should be checked and verified. I will at this point refer the reader to "The Idiot's Guides Beginning Investing", by Danielle L. Schultz. He describes the various US pension options much better than I can. Also it may be a chance to review an opposing view on investing.

Having said that, I suggest one take advantage of a company Roth 401(k) if available, if not an employer 401(k), then a Roth IRA and finally an Individual IRA, in that order.

A Roth 401(k) is an employer-sponsored investment savings account that is funded with after-tax dollars up to the plan's contribution limit. This type of investment account is well-suited to people who think they will be in a higher tax bracket in retirement than they are now. The traditional 401(k) plan is funded with pretax money, which results in taxes on future withdrawals. The 2019 contribution limit is $18,500. Workers age 50 and older can add an extra $6,000 per year in "catch-up" contributions, bringing their total to $24,500.

An Employer 401(k) is a retirement savings plan sponsored by an employer. It lets workers save and invest a part of their paycheck **before taxes** are taken out. There is a contribution limit, $18,500 for 2019. Taxes aren't paid until the money is withdrawn from the account.

A *Roth IRA* is a special retirement account that you fund with after-tax income (you can't deduct your contributions on your income taxes). Roth IRA contribution limit is $6,000 in 2019. The age 50 catch-up limit is fixed by law at $1,000 in all years.

An Individual Retirement Account (IRA) is a government sponsored, tax-deferred personal retirement plan. Taxes on Traditional IRA contributions and earnings are deferred until the account owner takes a distribution from the IRA. When money is withdrawn from a Traditional IRA it is taxed as regular income. The limit on annual contributions is $6,000 for 2019.

Non-registered accounts:

Finally, if you can, feel free to invest in low-yield, high-growth DG stocks through non-registered accounts. It's important to remember that the dividends in the non-registered accounts are taxed, though at a lower rate than regular income, so try and keep the dividend income low and go for price growth. The need for a non-registered account might arise if you have maxed out all other accounts. If you originally opened a DRIP, I would not close that account, but leave it, or even continue to add to it as there are no fees to do so.

Other Investments:

Other than Dividend Growth stocks, fixed income, ETFs and mutual funds, I will take this opportunity to mention some other popular investments, such as:

REITs:

> Real Estate Investment Trusts. These usually offer higher initial yields, but not always. They payout most of the company's earnings, thereby avoiding taxes, which are passed on to the people who buy the shares.
>
> Most of their earnings are paid out, so there is limited earnings growth, distribution (dividend) increases and price growth, if any. Here are five REIT examples showing their yearly distributions, 10-year dividend percentage growth rate and price charts (for 3).

Apply our three-rule test to any REIT (use Morningstar and The Dividend Channel) you are considering adding to your portfolio. Don't get excited by their higher yields, as there is little, if any, dividend and price growth, as shown in the three charts provided. Most REITs, in my opinion, fall into

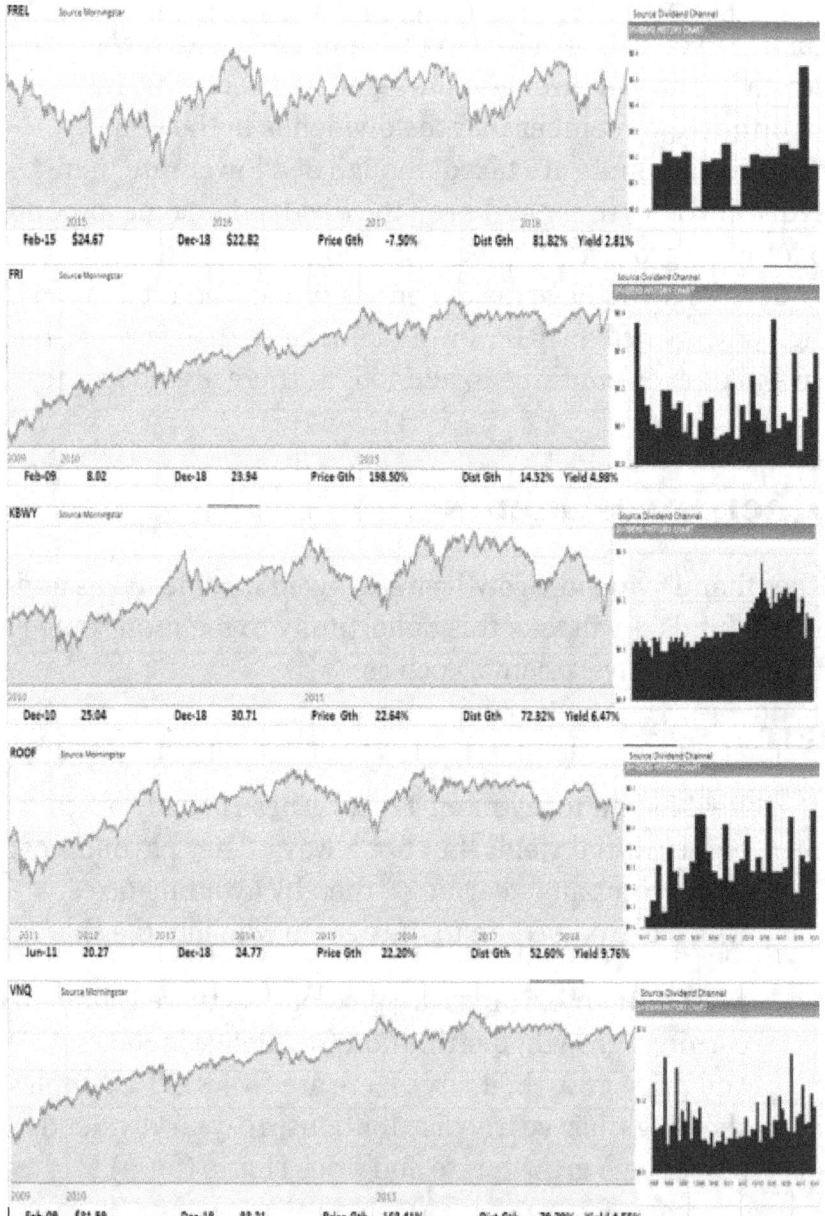

the high-yield, low growth investments. However, should you still wish to own some, buy them in the registered accounts to avoid paying taxes?Top 5 REIT's for 2018:

British ADRs:

2008	2009	2010	2011	2012	2013	2014	2015	2016	2017	2018	Div Gth
AZN	0.95	1.04	1.21	1.35	1.43	1.40	1.40	1.40	1.40	1.40	47.37%
ABB	0.45	0.43	0.47	0.67	0.70	0.72	0.77	0.77	0.75	0.76	68.89%
BBL	1.64	1.66	1.82	2.20	2.28	2.36	2.48	1.56	1.08	1.96	19.51%
BCS	0.00	0.00	0.00	0.00	0.00	0.00	0.00	0.00	0.00	0.00	0.00%
BP	3.30	3.36	0.84	1.68	1.98	2.19	2.34	2.40	2.40	2.40	-27.27%
BT	0.82	0.15	0.34	0.36	0.42	0.48	0.57	0.64	0.74	0.76	-7.32%
BTI	0.66	0.92	1.06	1.19	1.33	1.41	1.45	1.52	1.56	2.19	231.82%
CAJ	104.46	111.26	126.20	142.34	198.38	132.22	140.81	157.32	155.10	165.73	58.65%
CX	6.40	0.00	0.00	0.00	0.00	0.00	0.00	0.00	0.00	0.00	-100.00%
DEO	1.39	1.49	1.56	1.63	1.82	2.00	2.16	2.30	2.37	2.60	87.05%
GSK	1.13	1.20	1.29	1.35	1.47	1.56	1.60	1.57	1.55	1.61	42.48%
HMC	66.18	46.54	65.09	70.18	73.31	82.02	85.14	90.81	67.10	101.17	52.87%
HSBC	4.65	1.70	1.70	1.95	2.05	2.40	2.45	2.50	2.55	2.55	-45.16%
IHG	0.60	0.60	0.61	0.72	0.84	0.89	0.92	1.00	1.03	0.98	63.33%
INFY	0.04	0.06	0.07	0.09	0.08	0.10	0.15	0.19	0.19	0.22	450.00%
LYG	1.34	0.00	0.00	0.00	0.00	0.00	0.00	0.06	0.09	0.13	-90.30%
NGG	1.80	1.94	2.06	2.02	2.20	2.20	2.29	2.38	2.35	2.24	24.44%
NOK	0.50	0.41	0.31	0.39	0.19	0.00	0.11	0.14	0.26	0.17	-66.00%
NVO	0.64	0.88	1.09	1.92	2.80	3.61	4.51	5.04	9.33	7.58	1084.38%
NVS	1.54	1.71	1.95	2.36	2.48	2.53	2.72	2.67	2.72	2.72	76.62%
PKX	2230.45	2061.80	2427.77	2532.33	1950.57	2018.81	1997.03	1999.68	2077.31	2022.20	-9.34%
PNR	0.68	0.72	0.76	0.80	0.88	0.96	1.10	1.28	1.34	1.38	102.94%
RBS	11.15	0.00	0.00	0.00	0.00	0.00	0.00	0.00	0.00	0.00	-100.00%
RDS-B	3.12	3.32	3.36	3.42	3.56	3.72	3.76	3.76	3.76	3.76	20.51%
RIO	1.52	0.68	0.88	1.16	1.64	1.76	2.03	2.20	1.51	2.36	55.26%
SNE	35.40	25.47	31.89	27.56	26.60	24.93	0.00	19.82	19.10	27.17	-23.25%
SNN	0.25	0.27	0.29	0.32	0.41	0.52	0.87	0.60	0.63	0.61	144.00%
TSM	11.96	11.86	12.03	14.94	14.75	15.18	14.98	0.00	30.38	35.23	194.57%
UL	0.69	0.70	0.86	0.89	0.96	1.04	1.12	1.19	1.26	1.39	101.45%
VOD	1.69	1.63	1.92	2.77	2.23	2.29	1.34	1.56	1.39	1.48	-12.43%

These are British stocks which trade on the US stock market and pay their dividends in US currency. I still insist on applying our six-rule test to any other stock, than a Dividend Aristocrat, you may be interested in and did so to a group of 30 recommended British ADR stocks. The chart above shows the annual dividends and 10-year dividend growth rate of the 30 stocks. I disqualified 23 of the total 30 just using my 4-rule test alone. Here's the long-term dividend charts of the seven that met the three-rule test. How many would you keep? One or possibly two?

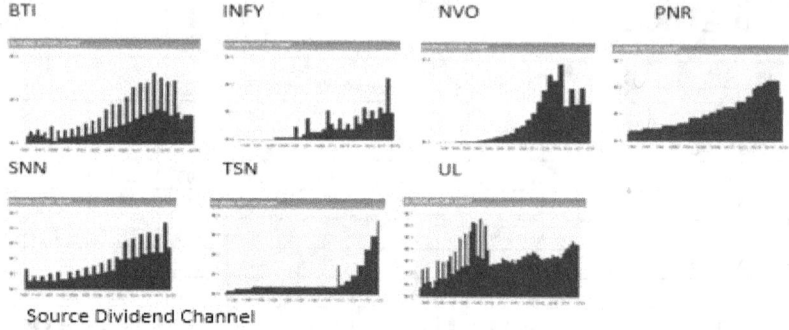

Source Dividend Channel

Also, many of the ADR stocks pay their dividend semi-annually, not quarterly, slowing the compounding.

It is always riskier to invest in foreign companies as it is harder to evaluate performance and gather information on the companies. I prefer companies I can confidently quantify.

I suggest sticking with companies you are familiar with, concentrating on US stocks many of which have extensive foreign investments. If you applied the three-rule test to the Dividend Aristocrats you will have found many had much higher 10-year dividend growth rates than these ADRs.

Gold:

Gold is usually considered a hedge against rapid inflation, however it pays no interest or dividends. If you wish to own gold buy the gold coins or bars from a bank or valid gold purveyor and consider it part of your savings or emergency funds. Do not consider gold as being part of your income investment.

When to sell your stocks?

Like Warren Buffett, a very high profile and respected figure in the financial community, I believe "***our favorite holding period is forever***". However, there are times when you should consider selling some or all of a company's shares:

- If you need the money.
- If the company cuts their dividend.
- If the company does not raise its dividend and you cannot justify holding the stock (it appears they will not raise it again soon),
- If you wish to get rid of stocks which have not performed as expected.
- If a major change effects the company (like a takeover), and you are more comfortable selling than waiting to see if the change is negative or positive.

I hope that you can see that you need to continue to hold your current roster of stocks to the same scrutiny that you applied when you first picked them. You should be monitoring the dividend payments, their increases and especially dividend growth rates of all stocks you own. Don't panic if there is negative news regarding one of your holdings, certainly monitor the news but as long as the monthly or quarterly dividends continue apace, and increase, there should be no reason to sell any of your stocks. The more information we have the better, but remember, we are not price-watching so we should not stress about the volatility of the market.

There is no denying that there are always investors that are looking for a better opportunity and cannot help but get caught up in "the next best thing". I wish them well in their pursuits, but personally, I'd rather keep holding on to my solid Dividend Growth performers, and sit back, relaxed, while my income continues to grow!

Personal note: When I was applying the three-rules to the stocks in preparation for this book, one of my own stocks did not make the list. I did not immediately move to get rid of this stock, rather I checked to ensure it continued to provide the income I expect, and it does. The purpose of the three-rule test is to compile a list of stocks to consider purchasing, it does not necessarily suggest shedding stocks the minute there is a questionable performance issue. This point is to demonstrate that regular assessment is key and provides an ease of mind that your money is always working towards the goals you have set.

Monitoring your portfolio:

> People who can manage their time can also manage their money. After all, managing minutes and managing money is the same exact principle. (Ann Marie Sabath, founder of Ease Inc.)

How should the income investor monitor their portfolio? Well, you will want to avoid a **"Stop-Loss System"**. Stop-losses are where one would set a sell price to minimize capital losses should the price of a stock drop. This may be a viable method for those investing for growth or buying and selling shares, but not for dividend growth investors.

For income investors, dividends are what we watch. Most quality dividend growth companies have a regular payment routine. For each quarter the board of directors announces the dividend to be paid the next quarter. However, those that raise their dividend usually do it the same quarter each year.

Knowing when companies pay and raise their dividend is the key. As long as they meet these pay dates and raise their dividend as expected, you can be assured that the company is in good shape. You don't need to scour the financial statements or listen to the expert opinions. The dividends should be so regular and consistent that you could set your calendar by their confirmation.

Making it easy to monitor an income portfolio:

As mentioned before, keeping track of the dividend growth percentage from one year to the next year is one of the most important aspects of monitoring your holdings.

The next section covers how to record your investment transactions. One of the more unrecognized advantages of monitoring your portfolio is the thrill of seeing your income grow. Every time your dividend payment is deposited in your accounts, you record it in your worksheets. I have never tired of reviewing my records and I have never lost the pleasure of having my investing decisions confirmed quarter after quarter. I hope you will enjoy this part of the process as much as I have!

Recording your investments:

I'm not referring to tracking the price of your holdings or how much your investments are worth. You can, if you wish, but what you really want to monitor is your income and the income growth.

In order to really appreciate income investing you must track the income your stocks are producing. It's not going to be sudden jumps upward, but a slow and gradual increase over time.

```
STOCKS:
HENRY'S\IRA CASH
HENRY'S\IRA STOCKS
  SUB-TOTAL HM IRA

HENRY Roth IRA CASH
HENRY Roth IRA STOCKS
  SUB-TOTAL HM Roth STOCKS

RAE'S IRA CASH
RAE'S IRA STOCKS
   SUB-TOTAL RM IRA

JOINT CASH
JOINT STOCKS VALUE

  TOTAL JOINT STOCKS

RAE'S Roth IRA CASH
RAE'S Roth IRA STKS
  SUB-TOTAL RM Roth IRA
```

I use an accounting program because I was an accountant and I like to account for the pennies. Excel provides the details and I'll present you with a quick sketch of the reports I've set up and how they work.

I also use an accounting program, like Quickbooks, where I've set up accounts for each account (IRAs, Roth IRAs & Non-Registered), examples are at the left:

All entries are made in the cash accounts, which record deposits, purchases, reinvestments and fees. **The cash account should always balance with the broker cash balance in your accounts.**

In the cash account, most transactions including commissions are coded to the matching stock account (Roth IRA cash entries are coded to Roth IRA stocks, and so on). The only transactions coded elsewhere are the account fees that are not related to stock purchases/sales. The sub-total accounts are my total investment in each category. I then use an Excel worksheet with several sub-worksheets where I re-enter the same transactions, but it provides the specific details on each stock and includes many more reports to record and track the income and summarize my holdings.

If you don't have or use an accounting program, then you would want an "Activity" worksheet in Excel. You would record each transaction in the various accounts you hold with the broker. This is how you will verify the cash balance in Excel with the cash balance in the broker's accounts. One

	Transaction Activity Report				
Date	Activity	Shares	Price	Amount	Balance
1-Jun-18	Deposit Funds			50.00	3,000.00
27-Jun-18	Bought	59.0121	42.1956	-2,500.00	500.00
28-Jun-18	Div			47.27	547.27
10-Jul-18	Bought	1.1561	25.1100	-29.03	518.24
13-Jul-18	Bought	2.1183	12.1700	-25.78	492.46
13-Jul-18	Div			51.12	543.58

always needs a cross-check when working with Excel to ensure the figures are correct.

- The last column, "Balance", is the amount which should match the broker's cash balance when you've made all entries.
- The cash balance of each account would appear on the Summary report, which is where you balance the shares and cash to the broker account.

You would then record the transaction (buying, dividends reinvested or selling) in an individual stock worksheet. The left side is to record New Purchases, the right side is for reinvested dividends. Sales would be negative entries.

The totals at the bottom would be linked to the Summary report (the amounts/figures will automatically show in the Summary).

Here is a sample of an individual stock transaction entry worksheet:

Sample Stock 1

Settlement Date	Action	Number of Shares	Price Per Share	Comm Fee	Number of Share Bal	ACB (Investment)	ACB per Share	Capital Gain (Loss)	Dividend Shares
3-Mar	Buy	100	$50.00	$10	100	$5,010.00	$50.10	–	0.00
1-May	Sell	-50	$120.00	$10	50	$2,505.00	$50.10	3,485.00	0.00
18-Jul	Buy	50	$130.00	$10	100	$9,015.00	$90.15	0.00	0.00
25-Sep	Sell	-40	$90.00	$10	60	$5,409.00	$90.15	-16.00	0.00
26-Sep	Div	1	$98.00	$0	61	$5,507.00	$90.28	0.00	1.00
27-Sep	Div	1	$120.00	$0	62	$5,627.00	$90.76	0.00	1.00
					62	$5,627.00	$90.76	0.00	0.00
				Totals	62	$5,627.00	$90.76		2.00

Record your Buys, Sells and the Dividend Reinvestments, for each stock on a similar worksheet. I've separated the stocks by accounts, TFSA, RRSP/RRIF, Non-Registered and even DRIP accounts. I've allowed for 10 stocks in each category. You add additional one, but you'll have to add them to the Summary report, in the right section and adjust the formulas.

Here's part of a Summary Report (a sample):

					Portfolio Summary Report				
TFSA Stocks	Adj Cost Base	ADC Per Share	Dividend Shares	Bought Shares	Number of Shares	DIV	Yearly Div	Ave Yield	Qtr
1st	$5,627.00	$90.76	$2.00	$60.00	62.0000	3.60	$223.20	3.97%	
2nd	#DIV/0!	#DIV/0!	0.0000	$0.00	0.0000	1.00	$0.00	#DIV/0!	
3rd	#DIV/0!	#DIV/0!	0.0000	$0.00	0.0000	1.00	$0.00	#DIV/0!	
4th	#DIV/0!	#DIV/0!	0.0000	$0.00	0.0000	1.00	$0.00	#DIV/0!	
5th	#DIV/0!	#DIV/0!	0.0000	$0.00	0.0000	1.00	$0.00	#DIV/0!	
6th	#DIV/0!	#DIV/0!	0.0000	$0.00	0.0000	1.00	$0.00	#DIV/0!	
7th	#DIV/0!	#DIV/0!	0.0000	$0.00	0.0000	1.00	$0.00	#DIV/0!	
8th	#DIV/0!	#DIV/0!	0.0000	$0.00	0.0000	1.00	$0.00	#DIV/0!	
9th	#DIV/0!	#DIV/0!	0.0000	$0.00	0.0000	1.00	$0.00	#DIV/0!	
10th	#DIV/0!	#DIV/0!	0.0000	$0.00	0.0000	1.00	$0.00	#DIV/0!	
Total TFSA	#DIV/0!		2.0000	60.0000	62.0000		$223.20	#DIV/0!	
Un-Invested	$0.00								

Look at the "1st" line and see that the figures match the Transaction totals above.
When the annual dividend paid by the "**Div**"

"Number of Shares" column MUST match with the number of shares in your broker account for each stock. If out, check your individual stock entries.

Notice the tabs at the bottom. The RRSP and TFSA are the other sub-worksheets which is where you actually record the transactions.

These two reports, Transaction and Summary, are the key reports in my Excel worksheets. You can design many other worksheets to provide specific information to track your own stocks or use them to provide the information that's important to you. I cannot express how handy I find Excel for tracking my investments. However, if you are not as familiar with Excel, I hope you can learn to use it, even if you only have a very elementary understanding of a basic worksheet. (Or, perhaps you could have a friend, or your kids or even your grandkids help you out). You may have your own method of recording, so my explanation is brief. Here is reminder that you can download samples of my Excel worksheets to help you get started:

You can Download my "Cdn Stock ACB Report Summary" Excel worksheet at:

https://drive.google.com/drive/u/1/folders/1kD-ZtK7WkIINobzB3HYJ1tnwnh9P3NDf

The sample worksheet includes:

- Summary Report
- TFSA: Stock Transaction worksheet - 10 stocks
- RRSP: Stock Transaction worksheet - 10 stocks
- Non-Reg: Stock Transaction worksheet- 10 stocks
- DRIP: Stock Transaction worksheet - 10 stocks
- Yield Projection

- Dividend Growth (DivGth) Calculation
- 10-Yr Average Yield (%Gth Yld) Calculation
- TSX 60 Listing & Exercise sheet
- NOBL Listing & Exercise sheet
- ACB Sample
- And others

NOTE:
1. The Adjusted Cost Base (ACB) for each stock will be calculated with each transaction.
2. The ACB per share is also show.
3. Capital Gains or Losses are shown when all or a portion of your stocks are sold.
4. Remember to update the annual dividend paid, when a company increases or cuts their dividend.
5. Save your worksheet every time you make entries.
6. Save the worksheet, under a different name at the end of each month, or for sure at the end of each year.

Again, whether you use my sample reports or your own, it is extremely important to **backup** your worksheets often. At year-end I always make a backup copy and name it: 2020_12 Stock Summary (for easy reference). When you make the next years' entries, it will change the totals and you will not be able to see certain data from the previous year-end. By having a backup each year you will be able to go back to see how the previous year ended.

I promise that once you've used Excel for a while making the entries will become easy and fast. I probably spend less than 20 minutes a week making entries, but spend more time watching the changes each entry has on my total income. Some would say watching paint dry is faster, but I argue, it's definitely not as satisfying!

Forget the basic rules of investing:

I doubt there are many investors, advisors and investing books which do not recommend or at least consider Diversification, Asset Allocation and Rebalancing as basic and sound investing rules. Their main objective is to protect the investor's capital and limit investor's risk. Sound advice and who would disagree?

In the Foreword, Tom Connolly said, "As you are most likely just beginning with dividend growth, some of what you encounter may have to be taken on faith for a while. It is truly unbelievable."

I also mentioned at the beginning, "We're not going to play their game of needing to beat the market, rather, we'll play our own game, with our own rules, ignoring the market altogether". Going against the basics of Investing 101: diversification, asset allocation and rebalancing, is where I ask you to take me on faith or at least consider my reasoning. If you see the merit in what I've presented so far, I hope that as I continue, you'll see how, "breaking the rules" is actually how you "beat the game". That I differ from traditional investing strategies is the key to achieving our objective: generating a growing income from our investments.

In this section, I will define these terms, and provide explanations why they don't necessarily work within my income investment strategy parameters.

Diversification:

Common definition: "Diversification is a technique that reduces risk by allocating investments among various financial instruments, industries, and other categories. It aims to maximize return by investing in different areas that would each react differently to the same event."

Rather than argue the point, I'll quote Warren Buffett:

> "Diversification is protection against ignorance. It makes little sense if you know what you are doing."

In other words, if you don't have the knowledge, time or know-how to identify quality investments, then covering all your bases might be a good way to go. However, you now have the three-rule test to quickly identify quality companies not just in the US, but in Canada and any other market. There is no need to dilute your holdings, lower your potential income or settle for below-average income returns.

Stick with large, stable and profitable companies with a long record of returning profits to its shareholders. I believe it relieves you of having to rely on diversification to mitigate market fluctuations. Diversify by selecting among the best stocks in every sector and in different markets. I'll repeat here that I prefer quality over quantity.

Another thing most forget is that during severe market corrections, recessions and crashes, ALL investments drop in value. The financial crisis of 2008 saw the market value of most portfolios drop by 35% or more. This included dividend growth portfolios. However, the difference was that dividend growth income investors did not see their income drop, though, to be fair, it grew at a slower rate. Fixed income was no protection, as interest rates dropped as well. There was a silver lining for the DG income investor, actually all investors, as the severe drop in prices was a great opportunity to buy more shares at depressed prices. DG investors would have benefitted the most as they are not worried when prices would rise, in fact they prefer them to stay down longer, enabling them to earn even more income!

For those thinking of diversifying into foreign stocks, or Emerging or International ETFs, I suggest you consider the many US companies with exposure to foreign markets, like McDonald's, Procter & Gamble and Coca-Cola. Like international stocks, they generate the bulk of their income outside the US. Buying shares of US multinationals can be an effective way for investors to get exposure to the global economy with quality DG companies. They are all listed in the Dividend Aristocrats list, but still they should be carefully assessed before purchasing.

Asset Allocation:

Common Definition: "Asset allocation is an investment strategy that aims to balance risk and reward by apportioning a portfolio's assets according to an individual's goals, risk tolerance and investment horizon. The three main asset classes - equities, fixed-income, and cash and equivalents - have different levels of risk and return, so each will behave differently over time."

As an income investor, bonds, preferred stocks and other fixed assets would not make up any part of your investment portfolio. Our objective is for a growing income, not a fixed one. Fixed assets may have a place as part of one's savings or funds, often set aside for emergency or other needs, but they are not effective in growing one's income, which is our priority.

I recommend you maintain a 100% equity income investment portfolio of the best dividend growth stocks which you will have chosen after careful evaluation.

Rebalancing:

Common Definition: "The primary goal of a rebalancing strategy is to minimize risk relative to a target asset allocation, rather than to maximize returns. A portfolio's asset allocation is the major determinant of a portfolio's risk-and-return characteristics. Yet, over time, asset classes produce different returns, so the portfolio's asset allocation changes. Therefore, to recapture the portfolio's original risk-and-return characteristics, the portfolio should be rebalanced."

As an income investor we make every attempt to reduce risk, in advance, by screening out stocks which do not meet our criteria. I feel very confident with my three-rule test, even providing for exceptions to those rules in order to find the best possible dividend growing stocks we can. The objective is to maximize income regardless of how the market reacts or other assets perform over time.

Bonds and fixed income assets, again, play no part in our income investment. I do recommend holding cash reserves and keeping savings separate from your investments. Once you've taken the time to research and build your income investment portfolio, the only time you should consider rebalancing is if you reevaluate a company's performance and find it fails to meet your expectations.

If your current roster of companies continues to provide the income growth you expect, and its future looks bright, there is no reason to divest yourself of any of your current shares.

We want to maximize our income and avoid giving up our best holdings. If you want to increase your holdings of a particular stock or sector, buy those on your next purchase.

I also don't feel it's important to maintain an even percentage between all stocks or sectors. I don't recommend you have all your holdings in a very small number of stocks or a single sector, but I do subscribe to the motto everything in moderation. Again, it's the income that is important and if you've built up a sizable holding of one company because you were able to buy it at a value-price, all the better. Never sell a good stock that keeps paying and growing your income.

Don't be swayed by the plethora of investment advice touting diversification, asset allocation and rebalancing. Trust your instincts, as I have, and resist the urge to "muck around" with your portfolio. Let others buy and sell to their heart's desire, all in the hopes of keeping their portfolios evenly distributed. I don't object if they do, it's just that I have learned through experience what suits my income goals and what is best for my investment portfolio.

The three "S's" of income investing

Simple: Income investing is one of the simplest forms of investing. By using the three-rule test to screen stocks you eliminate the lower quality dividend growth stocks. Evaluating company's past performance and deciding which stocks to add to your "List of stocks to consider" becomes a simple process. Once you've compiled your own List of stocks to consider, deciding which stocks to buy and when will be determined by the income the stocks will provide.

Sure: Income investing is a sure way to generate a growing income regardless of how the market reacts. By sticking with companies that have grown their earnings for long periods and regularly paid out a portion to shareholders, makes those future payments almost a certainty. By reinvesting the dividends you receive, you will generate income even if you stop adding funds to your portfolio.

Safe: Yes, there are risks with investing, but large, stable dividend growth companies are possibly the safest stocks one can find. As the companies pay and grow the dividend your investment becomes safer the longer you hold the stocks. That's the double dip, you receive more income over time and the value of your holdings also rise because your stock price will rise.

Chapter 5

I don't earn enough to invest in stocks!

Saving entails sacrifice; maybe that's why it brings rewards. (Mauricio Chaves Mesén, 12 Laws of Great Entrepreneurs)

Would you turn down someone if they handed you $20? How about $50 every three months, or even better $500/quarter or more? For those who think they don't have any spare money to invest in stocks, I am here to tell you that it simply isn't true. If you have enough money to buy lunch a couple times a month, then you have enough to start investing in dividend growth stocks. No matter how much one earns (or how little), you can start on the path to an ever-growing income. Make the effort to start saving and I'll show you how to make money on every cent you invest.

Even with an initial investment of $50 per month you could start generating income within one quarter, and you will be surprised how quickly your income will grow. And if you make a continuous effort to save, your quarterly income will become $50, then $100 per quarter and even more as time progresses.

In the US there are investment brokers which allow one to buy company stocks commission free. In addition, there are also a few brokers which also allow one to buy a fraction of a share (they call it Stock Slices). I'll mention two of the larger brokers for you to consider:

1. Charles Schwab

Charles Schwab's program allows you to buy a slice of any stock listed in the S&P 500 with as little as $5 and you can buy up to 30 slices at a time. And like trades for regular shares, you'll be able to place your trades without a commission. You'll continue to be able to reinvest any dividends from your stocks into fractional shares of the same stock.

2. Fidelity

You can start with just $1 and buy shares stocks on U.S. exchanges. You'll still be able to purchase stocks with zero trading commissions, and you'll also be able to reinvest your dividends in more shares, even fractional shares.

Being able to buy a fraction of a share means that once you've opened an investment account, you can then invest as little as $5.00 and buy a fraction of a company share, commission free. Of course, I don't recommend limiting your investments to $5.00, but if that's all you can afford to save, then put it to work immediately, earning you an income. Then when you can afford to add a few more dollars, do so, and continue to grow your investment income.

Remember to instruct your broker to automatically reinvest any dividend payments you receive, earning you even more income.

I have $1,000 and more to invest. Now what?

If you find a stock you like, buy a few shares to Test the Water. Wait a while and see how the stock does and if you still like it buy a bit more. By investing regularly, one would Average Up when prices were rising and Average Down when prices fell. In the long-term your Average cost should always be lower than the current price. (John Bart, founder of ShareOwners Investment Inc.)

....

It's not which dividend growth stock you buy, but when you buy it. (Tom Connolly, The Connolly Report)

If you are ready to invest larger amounts, you will need to open a discount investment account with a broker to purchase shares. See Appendix F for a partial list of discount brokers. If you can invest $1,000, $2,000, $5,000 or more, the DRIP process will seem cumbersome and restricting by not being able to buy immediately or at the price you wish.

A $1,000 investment will cost about a $6.95 commission, or .0695%, of the total investment with most discount brokers (6.95/1000 x 100). $2,000 will cost a 0.3475% fee and $4,500 a 0.154% fee. I'd suggest you try to keep the commissions to less than the 0.50%, always remember that the more money you can invest the lower your commission.

Even if you have larger sums to invest don't be tempted to expand your selection of your List of Stocks to Consider. Stick to the quality DG stocks you created from the Dividend Aristocrats using the three rules. If you find other stocks of interest run them through the six-rule test and add them to your list before buying. Invest in individual dividend growth stocks and avoid ETFs, Bonds, preferred stocks and mutual funds. I feel very strongly that these other products will dilute your position rather than enhance it. Build your holdings up slowly and over time. The thing to remember is that we are not playing the "price" game, rather the "income" game. What you want is to buy your stocks at a reasonable price, ones that give you the best yield for a stock. Once you actually buy, forget the price. The market constantly shifts, as will the price of a stock and that is what we are trying to avoid, the anxiety of market-watching. It's not that price isn't important, as I explained earlier in the book, it just isn't our priority.

Refer back to "How, where and what to invest" when deciding which account to use to purchase your stocks. I believe you should max out your Roth IRA, then the IRA, or company IRAs. My reasoning is that your account needs usually match your current income situation. As your income grows you'll probably be able to max out all three accounts and then look at adding funds to a non-registered account.

Again, depending on how much you have to invest, spread your investment over one or two stocks, keeping your commission low.

I already have a portfolio of ETFs and growth stocks, why change?

If you are content with your portfolio's performance than why consider a change? Good question, but I believe there are several good reasons to consider switching to dividend

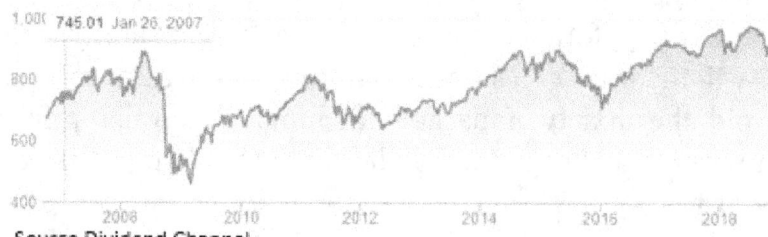

Source Dividend Channel

growth income investing:

1. If your portfolio consists mainly of ETFs and growth stocks, then your portfolio value is dependent upon the market and stock prices. Since the financial crisis, the market has generally been on an upswing. However, from its peak in June 2008, the market took until August 2014 (6 years) to recover from its 2009 low. That's how long it would have taken the value of your ETFs and growth stocks to recover.

2. It is worth asking yourself a number of questions: How much income is your current portfolio generating? How much has that income grown since 2008? If you consider some of the income growth examples we have provided, how does your income compare? Again, if you are dependent on market value, you now see the perils of traditional investing and hopefully, the advantages of income growth.

3. What do you think the value of your portfolio will be when the next major correction or crash occurs and how long might it take for your portfolio to recover? If you are like me, it is not a risk worth hanging my financial security on.

4. Would you expect the income from your portfolio to remain the same or even grow if there is a major correction? Even as I write this book, the market is extremely volatile, there is regular speculation on recession. This is stress you can avoid if you stop being dependent on price growth.

5. Even with a healthy portion in fixed assets, look at average CD interest rates and inflation from 2007 to 2018. Couple that with a 40% to 50% drop in stock prices and ask yourself how secure will your retirement income be when the next correction occurs? It is worth noting that drops in markets are advantageous to growth income investing, as much as it is for other forms of investing.

	Est. Average GIC Rates	Inflation
2018	1.25%	2.20%
2017	1.00%	1.56%
2016	1.00%	1.50%
2015	1.00%	1.61%
2014	1.05%	1.47%
2013	1.05%	1.24%
2012	1.35%	0.83%
2011	1.30%	2.30%
2010	1.05%	2.35%
2009	1.20%	1.32%
2008	2.00%	1.16%
2007	2.70%	2.38%

I have not given specific reasons for you to consider changing strategies, as I don't have all the answers to the questions. What I do know is that we can predict with some certainty that there will be a major market correction in the future and likely the effect on one's portfolio will be similar to the effects of past corrections.

However, if one focuses on income and an income growth method of investing, regardless of market fluctuations, your income should continue to grow, even if one's portfolio value decreases. This I know for a fact, I experienced this myself during the last major financial crisis. Both strategies can take advantage of low prices to buy more shares, but income investors will reap a double benefit when the market recovers, with price gain and lots of additional income.

You cannot control the value of your holdings, any more than you can control the market, but don't you think it would be nice to see consistent income growth, no matter how the market performs?

How do I switch to Income Investing?

If you do wish to switch to income investing, from ETFs and growth stocks, I suggest you "Bite the Bullet" on any ETFs or mutual funds you hold immediately. Sell them even if it means taking a loss. With the growth stocks you will want to select your own time to sell. If you already have a gain than sell right away, if not, you could hold to see if the market rises and sell at a break-even or at a profit. If they have performed badly you might just need to sell and chalk the loss up to "experience".

Don't just buy any stock I have mentioned in this book or ones recommended by others without first developing your own List of Stocks to Consider. Take the time to use the three-rule test and select from the stocks on your own list. Again, don't worry about owning all the stocks, but try to buy those which are value-priced and offer a reasonable yield. Build your portfolio over time. Add new stocks in different sectors and seek the best not the most, remember, quality or quantity.

I don't need the money. So why change my investments?

In investing, what is comfortable is rarely profitable.
(Robert Arnott, portfolio manager, PIMCO All Asset)

There are seasoned investors, comfortable with their current investment strategy, probably with a 60/40 portfolio of investments, with CDs, bonds and mutual funds. Content with the returns and satisfied with their current money flow, finding the energy needed to start an income growth investment fund may seem hard to muster.

I do have personal experience with such a person, someone who is retired, has a company pension, government pension, and was reluctant to change things up. They had cash savings of $35,000, mutual funds and CDs of $575,000 in registered accounts, drawing down $5,000/year from CDs to cover expenses. Annual interest earned on investments was $16,000 or 2.8%.

However, because of the financial crisis in 2008, the mutual funds dropped in value and CD rates were also low. This was enough for the person to ask for help to set up an income portfolio (we had discussed it several times in the past).

In 2015, here's what transpired:

- Opened an investment account at the bank with a registered accounts and Non-registered account.
- Sold the mutual funds and cashed in the CDs without losing the interest.

- Invested in nine DG stocks. Three in a DRIP so the dividends would be deposited into a savings account monthly (generating about $6,000 per year).
- As other CDs matured, the money was invested in DG stocks.
- In 2017 sold a REIT and an agriculture stock which had cut their dividend. Funds reinvested.
- Reinvested all dividends.
- No other activity, such as selling, to rebalance.

Today, in 2018, there are eleven DG stocks in the registered, Non-Registered and DRIP accounts. The DRIP now deposits $9,000 to the savings account, with no additional funds or stocks added, and the portfolio value (not market value) is now $650,000, generating $35,000 of dividend income or 5.38% (35,000/650,000 x100) per year. In three years, this person's annual investment income has doubled, and the income is no longer at the whim of the market. Not bad, I'd say!

They even began making the entries, recording the income and monitoring the increases. They still only need a very small amount of their investment to live on and are now planning on how to pass on their ever-growing income and investments to their beneficiaries. The person no longer worries about the market or price risks and expressed this opinion afterwards; "I wish I had done this years ago!"

Chapter 6

As an investor's time horizon lengthens equities become progressively less risky than bonds. (Warren Buffett, Letter, April 2018)

The proof is in the numbers:

The return on equities is equal to the current dividend yield plus dividend growth (plus or minus any valuation effect. (Buttonwood, The Economist)

Over the course of the book, I've made several statements and presented a system of investment that many might disagree with. One might have been wary of the contents of this book from the title, a lofty promise, an ever-growing income. After reading this far, I hope I have made the process of dividend growth investing clear, understandable, and most importantly, attainable.

But to be even more convinced, you might also be asking how much income can one earn from an income investment strategy?

It depends upon how much you are willing to invest and over what time frame. So, the answer is up to you, but look at the examples we've provided and the income growth rates. They have averaged a 10% compounded increase each year and with additional funds being added, you will accelerate the growth. So, it is very conceivable your income could grow to exceed your future annual expenses. I will always recommend that you save as much as you can, meeting your account maximums in as many cases as possible.

Let's go back to my grandson's figures presented in Chapter 1, where I showed how much income he earned each year. Maybe you were not impressed with the original dividend income figures. I've re-calculated what his income would have been if the funds were deposited in a High Interest saving account or in the XIU ETF.

The chart below shows the difference dividends, dividend increases and compounding can make.

	Actual Div Income			High Interest Acct			XIU ETF	
Year	Div	% Gth		Div	% Gth		Div	% Gth
2008	$217.30			$191.00			$128.73	
2009	$253.81	16.80%		$95.17	-50.18%		$126.18	-1.98%
2010	$281.43	10.88%		$91.08	-4.29%		$135.35	7.27%
2011	$323.94	15.10%		$113.16	24.25%		$137.75	1.77%
2012	$379.31	17.09%		$106.44	-5.94%		$173.43	25.91%
2013	$431.32	13.71%		$105.14	-1.22%		$203.83	17.53%
2014	$481.32	11.59%		$106.49	1.29%		$225.77	10.76%
2015	$531.84	10.50%		$78.35	-26.42%		$249.90	10.69%
2016	$588.67	10.69%		$66.85	-14.68%		$189.72	-24.08%
2017	$655.52	11.36%		$73.72	10.28%		$267.25	40.87%
2018	$767.36	17.06%		$110.45	49.82%		$328.06	22.75%
Total	$4,911.82			$1,137.86			$2,165.95	
Tangerine	Diff	$3,773.96		331.67%				
XIU	Diff	$2,745.87		126.77%				

The interest paid by the High Interest account was reinvested, as were the distributions from XIU over the 11 years. Do you see the negative growth? Look at the difference investing in a quality DG stock makes, $3,773.96 more income and a whopping 331.67% difference over the saving account and $2,745.87 and 126.77% difference over XIU. That's income growth, compounding and what I call an ever-growing income!

Have you heard the phrase: "*Show me the money*," made famous by characters in the 1996 film Jerry Maguire? If you invest in fixed income or low growth investment products (i.e.: Bonds and ETFs), you'll be asking yourself, "where is the money?"

Let's look at an actual stock purchase example where larger amounts were invested over a short period of 4 years:

	Invested	Income	Tot Invest	Inc % Gth
2011	$13,300	$181	$13,481	
2012	$24,680	$1,390	$39,551	667.96%
2013	$50,000	$3,739	$93,290	168.99%
2014	$41,000	$5,711	$140,001	52.74%
2015	$0	$9,295	$149,296	62.76%
2016	$0	$10,162	$159,458	9.33%
2017	$0	$11,179	$170,637	10.01%
2018	$0	$12,360	$182,997	10.56%
Totals	$128,980	$54,017	$182,997	
Ave Yld of Purchases		5.00%		
2018 Dividends		$12,360		
Yld on Total Investment		6.75%	(12,360/182,997)x100	

No other funds were added to the stock after 2014, other than reinvesting the dividends. 2016 to 2018 are the three years where income growth is due to reinvesting the dividend and dividend increases. As with the other examples I have provided this stock is averaging 10% income growth each year. The other important figure is the Yield on Total Investment, which is showing 6.75%. The average yield on all purchases was 5% (ranging from 4.3% to 5.5% over the 8 years), yet the overall yield and income is growing slowly and steadily and will likely continue year after year.

In Chapter 2 we said if one begins DG investing at age 60, they would need to invest larger amounts. This example might show the income they could generate over a short time and the type of yield on their investment they could obtain.

TFSA Results (similar to a Roth IRA account):

This next section provides a 10-year history of dividend investing that I am very familiar with, it belongs to my wife and me!

First, I want to summarize how you can achieve a growing income (these are practices I adhere to and have described throughout the book):

1. Save money for your retirement, separate from savings or emergency funds.
2. Invest regularly and if possible, increase the amount you save over time.
3. Invest your savings in quality dividend growth stocks selected by using the three-rule step process I have provided.
4. Avoid investing in fixed income bonds, CDs and preferred stocks, low-income growth mutual funds, ETFs or high yielding stocks.
5. Reinvest all dividends to enhance compounding.
6. Be conscious of the tax effects of investing in various accounts and products.
7. Do not sell your stocks unless one of your holdings cuts their dividend or no longer meets your income criteria.
8. Do not watch or worry about the price of your holdings or their market value.

My wife and I invested the maximum amounts into these accounts each January for a total of $57,500 each since

2009. I hold four DG stocks and my wife 5. All of our stocks are solid dividend growers, selected using the 4-rule test. Here's our 10-year summary:

Hm Tfsa	Orig Invest	Div (Inc)	% Gth	Orig + Div	Running Tot	Yield
2009	5,000.00	144.94		5,144.94	5,144.94	2.82%
2010	5,000.00	399.00	175.29%	5,399.00	10,543.94	3.78%
2011	5,000.00	862.35	116.13%	5,862.35	16,406.29	5.26%
2012	5,000.00	959.70	11.29%	5,959.70	22,365.99	4.29%
2013	5,500.00	1313.46	36.86%	6,813.46	29,179.45	4.50%
2014	5,500.00	1742.35	32.65%	7,242.35	36,421.80	4.78%
2015	10,000.00	2404.75	38.02%	12,404.75	48,826.55	4.93%
2016	5,500.00	3301.78	37.30%	8,801.78	57,628.33	5.73%
2017	5,500.00	3813.66	15.50%	9,313.66	66,941.99	5.70%
2018	5,500.00	4496.91	17.92%	9,996.91	76,938.90	5.84%
Totals	$57,500.00	$19,438.90			$76,938.90	

Rm Tfsa	Orig Invest	Div (Inc)	% Gth	Orig + Div	Running Tot	Yield
2009	5,000.00	129.82		5,129.82	5,129.82	2.53%
2010	5,000.00	399.00	207.35%	5,399.00	10,528.82	3.79%
2011	5,000.00	758.17	90.02%	5,758.17	16,286.99	4.66%
2012	5,000.00	1,116.20	47.22%	6,116.20	22,403.19	4.98%
2013	5,500.00	1,516.00	35.82%	7,016.00	29,419.19	5.15%
2014	5,500.00	2,182.03	43.93%	7,682.03	37,101.22	5.88%
2015	10,000.00	2,917.74	33.72%	12,917.74	50,018.96	5.83%
2016	5,500.00	3,661.32	25.48%	9,161.32	59,180.28	6.19%
2017	5,500.00	4,143.28	13.16%	9,643.28	68,823.56	6.02%
2018	5,500.00	4,750.65	14.66%	10,250.65	79,074.21	6.01%
Totals	$57,500.00	$21,574.21			$79,074.21	

	Original invest	Our 2018 Annual Div			Total with Div Reinvest	Yield on Invest
2018 Combined	$115,000.00	$9,247.56			$156,013.11	5.93%

The chart shows the contributions made to each account and summarizes the 10 years since it was started. Notice that the "Yield" column percentage, on the right (in each account) varies up and down each year, but gradually increases. There are several reasons for this:

1. The price of stock purchases varied.
2. The dividend increases varied.
3. We bought some higher yielding stocks, then sold them when they cut the dividend and eliminated some

that we felt would not provide the dividend growth we sought.

4. Stock prices may have fallen while the dividend increased.

The three columns I like to watch are:

- the gradual and continuous income growth each year,
- the "% Gth" (percentage growth) of the income year-over-year, and
- the "Yield" column, which is the yield on investment and is currently 5.93% for the combined yield of both accounts.

There is a Chinese proverb which says "one picture is worth ten thousand words". So let's look at a chart of me and my wife's actual TFSA (similar to a Roth IRA) income growth from 2009 to 2019 (which includes the financial crisis). As of 2019 our combined income will be just under $12,000.

WIFE & MY TFSA INCOME

We've achieved these results with the "Steady Eddies" mentioned earlier. None are speculative or high yield stocks (even the ones we sold), we invested the maximum, didn't try to time the purchases, but with confidence, we just sat back and let the process do its work.

There will always be new choices which appear to offer the same or better returns. New large US companies, ETFs, mutual funds, REITs and British ADRs. You will even see new bond offerings which seem appealing, like CoPower's Green private Bonds, with a 5% yield, and a 6-year fixed-rate. These products are designed to attract investors with their enticing rates, but you need to recognize that the rate is fixed and will not grow, while the others will just dilute your holdings. They offer short-term sparkle, but no long-term value.

Never forget, though, it is not in dividend stocks or high interest fixed-rates, but with dividend growth stocks you will achieve your goal.

I started this book in the middle of 2018 and made reference to Star Trek and my own solution to the Market Kobayashi Maru:

- An alternative to seeking market returns and eliminating the reliance on market returns.
- A system where your returns are not tied to price fluctuations and won't play a part in your investment decisions.

Little did I know that just as I finished I would be looking at the two following financial headlines on December 31, 2018:

"Stock Markets Worldwide Close Out Worst Year Since 2008" and

"US stocks post worst year in a decade as the S&P 500 falls more than 6% in 2018"

The Dow fell 5.6%%. The S&P 500 was down 6.2%. It was the worst year for stocks since 2008. Our own portfolio value was down 7.33% for 2018.

However, throughout this book I have insisted that we ignore the market and its effect on holdings and, instead, I have shown you, with all the account examples, that they have increased their income each year (actually more than 10% for 2018 despite the worst market performance since 2008). Our own portfolio income (actual dividends received) was up 10.72% over 2017. I imagine some skeptical of this strategy would think *"nice work if you can get it"*, but you can! Generate your own ever-growing income through diligence, patience and discipline, following the process described. Who wouldn't want an alternative to worrying if the market will continue its downward trend, if it recovers or goes sideways? Let others be concerned with market gyrations, income investors can ignore the market and smile as our income continues to grow.

It's the growing income from your dividend growth payers that should always remain your focus, as well as the growing yield. A growing yield indicates that you are earning more income with less money invested. In other words, "it costs you less to receive $1 dollar of income as time passes. Fixed income or low-growth products simply cannot provide you with the same steady income growth over time that comes from a growing yield.

This brings us to what has become my mantra, and conveniently the title of my book:

Your Ever Growing Income: The Rising Yield on investments

How much money do you need to save to retire?

A dividend growth retirement portfolio allows us to continue building wealth after retirement. (Tom Connolly, 2014)

Here is a suggestion by Michele Cagan, CPA, an author and financial mentor, on a method to calculate how much money you should save for retirement:

> *"To come up with how much you'll need to save, start with money that's guaranteed to come in during your retirement. Subtract the expenses you realistically expect to have. The difference between those numbers is the amount your savings will need to support every month. Multiply that monthly difference by 12 (to get a year's difference) and then by 25 or 30 – the number of years you expect to spend in retirement".*

- Michele Cagan, CPA

Here are a few examples of her suggested calculation:

Monthly Income	$3,000	$3,100	$3,200	$3,300	$3,400
Yearly Income	$36,000	$37,200	$38,400	$39,600	$40,800
Monthly Expenses	$4,600	$4,900	$5,200	$5,500	$5,800
Yearly Expenses	$55,200	$58,800	$62,400	$66,000	$69,600
Monthly Difference	$1,600	$1,800	$2,000	$2,200	$2,400
Yearly Shortfall	$19,200	$21,600	$24,000	$26,400	$28,800
30 Years Retirement	$576,000	$648,000	$720,000	$792,000	$864,000

Another common suggestion I have found is that you will need a portfolio of at least a million dollars or more before you can retire comfortably. When I was still seeking "experts" for financial advice I was given this rather astronomical goal as requirement for a secure financial retirement. $1 Million is often suggested because one can expect to generate approximately $40,000 of annual income (allowing for a basic 4% interest rate: $1Million x 4.0% = $40,000). Add government pensions or other guaranteed income, say $35,000 in total, and you arrive at a potential of $75,000 of annual income before taxes.

If you're wondering how one could even amass a $1 Million dollar portfolio, consider the following projection (and wonder if it is even achievable!) Consider saving $5,000 every year for 35 years and hope to earn an annual 8.5% rate of return. If possible here are the results:

Age	Actual Amount Invested	Market Value	Annual Return Each Year
30	$5,000.00	$5,425.00	8.50%
35	$25,000.00	$40,302.49	8.50%
40	$50,000.00	$92,746.25	8.50%
45	$75,000.00	$171,603.67	8.50%
50	$100,000.00	$290,178.15	8.50%
55	$125,000.00	$468,473.46	8.50%
60	$150,000.00	$736,568.40	8.50%
65	$175,000.00	$1,139,691.15	8.50%

The flaw with both of these scenarios is that they deal with an assumed guaranteed fixed rate of return over a long period of time. One would be wholly dependent on a consistent return, quite a high one at that, for decades at a time. Even worse, if one has a mix of fixed assets and equities, the fixed assets will provide a lower return requiring higher returns from the equities. Positive returns for 35 years from the stock market is just not possible and there are way too many variables to accurately estimate future expenses and inflation.

One key aspect of the Income Growth strategy, is that your yield on your total investment should grow. What that means is that as you invest more money in quality dividend growth stocks, it will cost you less, and less to earn a reasonable income as time passes.

Let's see how it actually might work. I'll assume you invested $6,000 every January beginning 2008 through to 2022 in Johnson & Johnson. Here are your results:

Year	Invested amounts	Income Earned	Income Gth % Each Yr.	Total Invested	Yield on Investment
2008	$6,000.00	$170.03		$6,170.03	2.76%
2009	$6,000.00	$390.50	129.67%	$12,560.53	3.11%
2010	$6,000.00	$638.38	63.48%	$19,198.91	3.33%
2011	$6,000.00	$933.80	46.28%	$26,132.71	3.57%
2012	$6,000.00	$1,253.03	34.19%	$33,385.73	3.75%
2013	$6,000.00	$1,610.57	28.53%	$40,996.31	3.93%
2014	$6,000.00	$1,954.95	21.38%	$48,951.26	3.99%
2015	$6,000.00	$2,077.16	6.25%	$57,028.42	3.64%
2016	$6,000.00	$2,427.92	16.89%	$65,456.33	3.71%
2017	$6,000.00	$2,846.23	17.23%	$74,302.56	3.83%
2018	$6,000.00	$3,239.14	13.80%	$83,541.70	3.88%
2019	$6,000.00	$3,722.67	14.93%	$93,264.38	3.99%
2020	$6,000.00	$4,620.20	24.11%	$103,884.58	4.45%
2021	$6,000.00	$5,148.86	11.44%	$115,033.44	4.48%
2022	$6,000.00	$5,764.51	11.96%	$126,797.95	4.55%
Total	$90,000.00	$36,797.95			
Total Investment		$126,797.95			
Yield on Investment		4.55%			

Beside the growing income earned each year, look at the last column. This is your yield on your total investments, which includes the reinvested dividends. The yield begins at just below 3%, but gradually grows. It may not grow every year, as there was a drop in 2015, but eventually it grew to 4.55% by the end of 2022. To determine your yield, divide the 2022 dividends by your total investment (5,764.51 / 126,797.95 = 4.55%).

If one assumed that $1Million is required to earn $40,000 of income, (1,000,000 x .04% = $40,000) how does a rising yield change that calculation?

Using the JNJ example above, if one continues investing in the company, but the yield remains 4.55%, you would require an investment of $879,852. But its likely, that your yield will continue to grow, and it is not unreasonable to expect your yield to grow to 6.0%, 7.5% and possibly higher.

Yield on Investment	Investment	Income
4.00% Yield on Investment	$1,000,000	$40,000
4.55% Yield on Investment	$879,852	$40,000
6.00% Yield on Investment	$666,667	$40,000
7.50% Yield on Investment	$533,333	$40,000

Should the yield grow to 6.0% you will only require $666,667 to earn $40,000, as the above charts shows.

$666,667.00 might seem high for one account, but most likely you will have other investments, such as an IRA, which will likely become the larger portion of your portfolio. The point is that if you invest with DG stocks throughout your entire portfolio, your yield on your entire portfolio will grow steadily and continuously. So, if $40,000 is your income goal and, if you invest wholly in DG stocks, it will take much less than one-million dollars to achieve financial freedom!

IMPORTANT I mentioned that our portfolio income rose 10.72% over last year, but I'd like to point out that we received that money for doing nothing. The companies paid us dividends, which were automatically reinvested and all of the companies raised their dividend during 2018, but we did not contribute a cent. Here's the most important takeaway from my entire investing philosophy, **when you invest in quality DG stocks to generate an income, the companies also contribute by paying you a dividend. You reinvest the dividends to buy more shares and increase your income. Finally, when the companies raise the dividend on all the shares you own it further grows your income. You continue to add funds and the process accelerates. In other words, they are helping you to grow your income by adding to what you contribute, so you don't need to save as much to reach your income goal!** That's how and why the yield on your investment rises. Please read this paragraph a few times so that you fully grasp its meaning.

I cannot stress enough the concept of the **Rising Yield**, because it's the key to earning enough income to retire without having to depend on selling your capital or needing to invest larger sums to obtain the same results. Those who invest for capital appreciation (the price rising) need and hope the price goes up continuously, which it never does. I'll again refer to our portfolio dropped in value by 7.33% in 2018. In order to get back to our 2017 value we need a 7.91% increase. The larger the drop the greater the increase needed to recover. A 50% drop will require a 100% increase to get back to the original value. No one wants to be a slave to the temperamental market, nervously watching price or having to worry about market performance, when you could be receiving a growing income regardless of price or the market.

To me, it's such a simple concept that I wonder why so few recognize it. *The longer you hold shares of solid*

dividend growth stocks, the greater your income and yield will become.

That's the point I am trying to get across with my book, if you invest regularly, reinvest the dividends, continue to buy more shares (the lower the price the better) and receive regular dividend increases, then there is no reason not to expect to retire with a steadily growing income to meet future needs. When you track your progress, as I have shown throughout the book, you will know long before you retire just how well you're doing. And if you're like me, you will gain a lot of comfort knowing your future is on its way to being financially secure. You won't be wondering "how much do I need to save", instead you will see your income steadily increase, encouraging you to save even more and invest in more solid DG stocks.

My friend Mark Seed, of the blog, *"My Own Advisor"* (https://www.myownadvisor.ca/), is a dividend investor and has set a retirement financial goal of $30,000/year from his investments, primarily through his dividend growth stocks. He updates his progress monthly and shows the progress yearly on a chart. He's well on his way and will likely achieve his goal sooner than projected. Mark is a great example of how successful this form of investing can be, with patience and dedication, even providing a path to early retirement!

I have not mentioned the large number of followers of Tom Connolly. They are the silent, contented, and extremely grateful group that we rarely hear from, who, like me, discovered dividend growth investing and are now reaping the benefits. After employing patience and persistence, they are just enjoying their retirement.

Although I am advocating a singular form of investing, one that seems counterintuitive to most popular forms of portfolio building, I am very confident that you can and will benefit from it in ways that other forms of investing cannot provide. Income investing does require patience, it's a long-haul form of income growth, but in the end, aren't we all looking for the same end goal? To have enough money to see us through retirement in financial security and comfort! I believe very strongly that if you set your own income goal and follow my lead, you will not worry about having to beat the market, or stress over annual returns. As your investment grows, so will your income at an increasing rate, especially if your yield is increasing. **Don't get side-tracked by trying to rush or speed things up by chasing yield.**

How much income do you need?

You can never have enough, if you ask me. There are four areas of concern which can affect every retirees income:

1. Company crisis

I read an article in the Financial Post, August 22, 2019 by Tom Bradley, here's a quote:

> "What do the bad outcomes look like? *Assume your stocks drop 25 per cent. What does this translate into in dollar terms? How does it feel to lose $250,000 on a million-dollar portfolio? And how will it feel if your income drops because a couple of holdings cut their dividends"?*

Dividend cuts are a possibility, even from companies which have paid and raised them for many years. It has happened in the past and I'm sure it will happen to other quality companies in the future. Dividend cuts by some stocks you own don't necessarily mean your overall income will drop. But those who invest for capital appreciation can't say the same about price drops. How long would it take to recover from a $250,000 drop in value? Some might never gain it back, especially if the market continued to drop and stayed down for a while.

2. Inflation

Inflation has been discussed, but too often over-looked. Should the economy turn for the worst, high inflation rates, like those experienced in the 1970s, may occur and often the increases happen quickly.

3. Life Changes

We all hope that as we age we have the opportunity to relax and enjoy our retirement years in general good health, but possible illness and physical impairment may require extensive care, possibly moving to a care facility or one might wish to use in-home care. All are expensive and they are not fixed costs.

4. Family Changes

Ideally we would like to believe that ones' family will be there to assist should help or support be needed, but too often the reverse is the case. Families become busy, move or there may even be a parting of the ways. Those of us who have the benefit of family support, when needed, should be extremely grateful.

We can't foresee the future and we know things can and will change, so the more income your investments generate the safer you and your financial status will be. Just keep to the same path and count on your growing income from you're your *Ever Growing Income" investment strategy.*

One last point: if you are a retired investor, regardless if your retirement dividends surpass your living expenses or not, you often hear recommendations to change your current investment strategy by increasing the fixed asset allocation.

Standard "advice" from financial advisors to retirees is to reduce your equity positions to bonds, or other fixed assets, ("you almost certainly want exposure to bonds in your portfolio, with your exact weighting tied to your age, risk tolerance, investing goals and such", Rob Carrick). So, if my wife and I were to follow such advice, we'd be 77% bonds or other fixed assets and giving up the larger portion of our growing income each year (10.72% for 2018) for a fixed income? Thanks, but no thanks!

Instead, I suggest that you stick to your dividend growth stocks in retirement, as we do, sit back and continue collecting those ever-rising dividends and a higher income each year.

Oh, did I mention one of the biggest advantages of this strategy? You'll look forward with joyful anticipation to receiving your dividend payment, and the joy you feel only increases as your dividends increase!

I opened with a Star Trek analogy. I hope you'll indulge me as I close with one.

Our mission: to explore strange new sources of income, to seek out quality, dividend growth companies, to boldly go where no other investing book has gone before (and guide you to your own path of an ever-growing income!)

The Five & Ten-Stock Income Growth portfolio

The Five-Stock Income portfolio:

This strategy is suitable for a beginner, a child's portfolio (could be in an adult's name), or even for one who is just looking for a simplified income growth portfolio.

Guidelines: Select one stock from five different sectors or categories which are listed in Appendix A Dividend Aristocrat Stocks, plus one stock which would be considered a Low yield/high growth.

How to invest:

It is recommended that you have an investment account with a broker which has commission free trading and allows for fractional share purchases

The first choice would be a Roth IRA account, secondly a Non-registered account.

Try to set up a specific monthly amount to invest ($50, $75, $100, or more).

Buy Fractional shares of the five stocks, in equal dollar amounts with your monthly contribution.

Set up automatic dividend reinvestment for the account.

Record the stock purchases and dividend reinvestments in the Excel worksheet.

When you can afford to, increase the monthly contributions.

There is no need to rebalance the holdings, or consider adding any other stocks.

Do not sell any of the stocks, unless one of the companies cuts the dividend.

If you did sell a stock, select a new stock in the same category, and use the funds to buy shares in the new stock.

With the Five-Stock portfolio, you will be investing on a regular basis, hopefully monthly, and applying dollar cost averaging (not worrying about the current price).

The Ten-Stock Advanced Income portfolio:

Guidelines: Select two stocks in five sectors, including two Low Yield/High Growth stocks, from the Dividend Aristocrat Stocks.

How to invest:

It is recommended that you have an investment account with a broker which allows for commission free, and Fractional share purchase.

The first choice would be a Roth IRA account, secondly a Non-registered account.

Set up the Yield Difference worksheet with the ten stocks listed by category, or sector.

Always buy Fractional shares.

When you have money to invest ($100, $500, $1,000 or more), enter the current price of each ten stocks into the Yield difference worksheet, and buy an equal amount of the stock in each category, with the highest yield difference.

Set up automatic dividend reinvestment for the account.

Record the stock purchases and dividend reinvestments in the Excel worksheet.

There is no need to rebalance the holdings, however, you can consider adding other quality stocks from a different sector.

If you do add new stocks, continue spreading your new investments equally between the stocks in each sector.

Do not sell any of the stocks, unless one of the companies cuts the dividend.

If you did sell a stock, select a new stock in the same category, and use the funds to buy shares in the new stock.

With the Ten-Stock portfolio, you are looking to buy stocks which offer a slightly higher yield, and you can decide when to invest (looking to buy during a market dip), or ignore current market price, and invest on a regular basis.

Select your stocks following the four-rule test described in this book.

Final Comments:

I'd like to take the opportunity to provide a list of lessons I've learned and important points to remember if you're seriously interested in starting this journey with income growth investing:

- A stock has no real value unless it pays a dividend.
- If a company does not pay a dividend, avoid, otherwise you are completely dependent on the price rising and your only return is when/if you sell the stock.
- It's not just which dividend stock, but which **dividend growth** stock to buy. Be conscious of what to buy and when. When stock prices go down, your stock purchases rise, and you will generate more retirement income.
- Dividend growth is about future earnings, not current earnings.
- Always require dividend growth year after year, this will lead you to finding high quality stocks (ones which have rising earnings year after year).
- Diversification is not the answer, instead concentrate on holding only quality dividend growth stocks.
- In the long-term, dividend growth encourages the price of the stock to grow.
- Let dividend yield and yield on investment be your benchmark, not whether your portfolio beats the market index.

Definitions:

Bond:

A fixed income investment where one lends money for a fixed interest rate for a set period of time. You can also purchase a Bond ETF, comprised of many bonds bundled together.

Dividends:

A part of a company's profits which are distributed to shareholders. Dividends may be in the form of cash or shares. Cash payments are paid out on a per share basis, ex: $1.20 per share, or $0.30 paid quarterly.

Dividend Payout Ratio:

The portion of earnings paid out as dividends to shareholders, typically expressed as a percentage. The payout ratio can also be expressed as dividends paid out as a portion of cash flow.

DRIP:

Dividend Reinvestment Plan. The cash dividends paid by a company are used to buy more shares of the company without any fees.

Earnings:

The earnings of a business are the same as its net income or its profit. Either term means the same thing. Earnings are usually calculated as all revenues (sales) minus the cost of sales, operating

	expenses, and taxes, over a given period of time (usually a quarter or a year).
Free Cash Flow	Free Cash Flow per share (FCF) is a measure of a company's financial flexibility and is determined by dividing free cash flow by the total number of shares outstanding.
Investment:	The action or process of investing money for profit.
P/E Ratio:	P/E is short for the ratio of a company's share price to its per-share earnings.
Portfolio	The total of your investments, which may include, cash, IRA, Roth IRA, Non-registered accounts, DRIP, physical Gold and other investments.
Share Certificate:	A written document that is signed on behalf of a corporation to serve as a legal proof of ownership of number of shares.
SPP:	Share Purchase Plan. One can invest additional funds to buy shares without having to pay a commission.

Stock (or Shares):	A share in the ownership of a company. Stock represents a claim on the company's assets and earnings.
Total Investment:	The total amount of financial resources that a person has in a project. Includes original investments, re-invested dividends and new funds added to a portfolio.
Yield	Is the annual dividend divided by the current share price of a stock.
Yield on Investment	Total portfolio dividends divided by the total investment (not market value) of your portfolio.

APPENDIX A

57 Dividend Aristocrat Stocks:

Ticker	Description	Sector
GD	GENERAL DYNAMICS CORP	Areospace
TROW	T ROWE PRICE GROUP INC	Asset Management
BEN	FRANKLIN RESOURCES INC	Asset Management
KO	COCA-COLA CO/THE	Beverage
PEP	PEPSICO INC	Beverage
BF/B	BROWN-FORMAN CORP-CLASS B	Beverage
ED	CONSOLIDATED EDISON INC	Elec Utility
NEE	NEXTERA ENERGY INC	Electrial Utility
XOM	EXXON MOBIL CORP	Energy
CVX	CHEVRON CORP	Energy
BRO	BROWN & BROWN INC	Financial
MCD	MCDONALD'S CORP	Food
MKC	MCCORMICK & CO-NON VTG SH	Food Processing
SJM	JM SMUCKER CO/THE	Food Processing
ABBV	ABBVIE INC	Health
JNJ	JOHNSON & JOHNSON	Health Supply
GWW	WW GRAINGER INC	Industrial Elec Equip
SWK	STANLEY BLACK & DECKER INC	Industrial Machinery
CHRW	C.H. ROBINSON WORLDWIDE INC	Industrial Service
CAT	CATERPILLAR INC	Industry
EMR	EMERSON ELECTRIC CO	Industry
ROP	ROPER TECHNOLOGIES INC	Industry
PNR	PENTAIR PLC	Industry
KVUE	KENVUE INC	Industry
GPC	GENUINE PARTS CO	Industry Auto Parts

LIN	LINDE PLC	Industry Chemical
APD	AIR PRODUCTS & CHEMICALS IN	Industry Chemical
ECL	ECOLAB INC	Industry Chemical
PPG	PPG INDUSTRIES INC	Industry Chemical
ALB	ALBEMARLE CORP	Industry Chemical
MMM	3M CO	Industry Diversified
HRL	HORMEL FOODS CORP	Industry Food
ADM	ARCHER-DANIELS-MIDLAND CO	Industry Food
PG	PROCTER & GAMBLE CO/THE	Industry Household
CHD	CHURCH & DWIGHT CO INC	Industry Household
CL	COLGATE-PALMOLIVE CO	Industry Household
KMB	KIMBERLY-CLARK CORP	Industry Household
CLX	CLOROX COMPANY	Industry Household
CTAS	CINTAS CORP	Industry Industrial
DOV	DOVER CORP	Industry Machinery
NDSN	NORDSON CORP	Industry Machinery
AOS	SMITH (A.O.) CORP	Industry Machinery
ITW	ILLINOIS TOOL WORKS	Industry Metal Fab
FRT	FEDERAL REALTY INVS TRUST	Industry REIT
ESS	ESSEX PROPERTY TRUST INC	Industry REIT
O	REALTY INCOME CORP	Industry REIT
WBA	WALGREENS BOOTS ALLIANCE INC	Industry Retail
NUE	NUCOR CORP	Industry Steel
SPGI	S&P GLOBAL INC	Information Services

EXPD	EXPEDITORS INTL WASH INC	Industrial Service
CB	CHUBB LTD	Insurance
AFL	AFLAC INC	Insurance
CINF	CINCINNATI FINANCIAL CORP	Insurance
ADP	AUTOMATIC DATA PROCESSING	IT Services
WST	WEST PHARMACEUTICAL SERVICES	Medical Supply
CAH	CARDINAL HEALTH INC	Medical Supply
BDX	BECTON DICKINSON AND CO	Medical Supply
MDT	MEDTRONIC PLC	Medical Supply
ABT	ABBOTT LABORATORIES	Medical Supply
ATO	ATMOS ENERGY CORP	Natural Gas
AMCR	AMCOR PLC	Packaging
WMT	WALMART INC	Retail
TGT	TARGET CORP	Retail
SHW	SHERWIN-WILLIAMS CO/THE	Retail Building
LOW	LOWE'S COS INC	Retail Building
IBM	INTL BUSINESS MACHINES CORP	Technology
SYY	SYSCO CORP	Wholesale Food

APPENDIX B

Dividend Aristocrat stocks offering DRIPs commission free share purchases:

As of this writing, there are eleven Dividend Aristocrat companies which offer commission-free investing to purchase additional shares:

Symbol	Company	Min	Max	Fee	Sh
MMM	3M Company	$10.00	$40,000.00	0	1
ABT	Abbott Laboratories	$25.00	$150,000.00	0	1
ABBV	AbbVie Inc.	$25.00	$150,000.00	0	1
AFL	AFLAC Incorporated	$50.00	$250,000.00	0	1
EMR	Emerson Electric Co	$25.00	$250,000.00	0	1
HRL	Hormel Foods Corp	$25.00	$80,000.00	0	1
ITW	Illinois Tool Works Inc.	$100.00	$120,000.00	0	1
JNJ	Johnson & Johnson	$25.00	$50,000.00	0	1
NUE	Nucor Corporation	$10.00	$12,000.00	0	1
SHW	Sherwin-Williams Co	$10.00	$12,000.00	0	1
XOM	Exxon Mobil Corporation	$50.00	$250,000.00	0	1

There are other quality companies which offer commission-free DRIPs, but I suggest you begin with the Dividend Aristocrats as I used them throughout this book as our initial analysis on those companies. Select the company or companies which made your List of Stocks to Consider.

APPENDIX C

Top five ETFs of 2018:

These are the top five ETFs out of 1929. I hope you can see

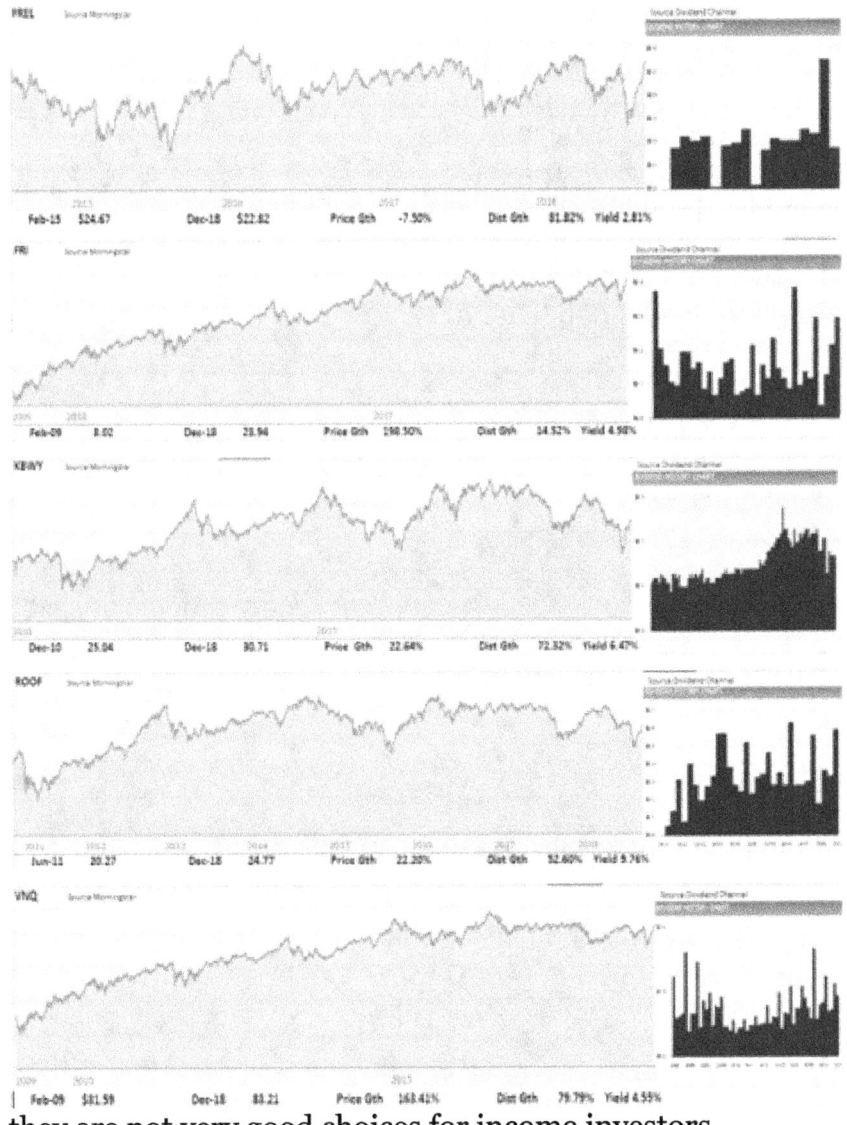

they are not very good choices for income investors.

APPENDIX D

Web sites recommended:

Morningstar home page:
http://portfolios.morningstar.ca/RtPort/Reg/AllView.aspx#780-hidenews

The Dividend Channel:
https://www.dividendchannel.com/history/?symbol=nobl

Sure Dividend:
https://www.suredividend.com/dividend-aristocrats-list/

Dividend History:
https://dividendhistory.org/

Recommended books:

The Investment Zoo, by Stephen A. Jarislowsky. Published by Transcontinental, 2009

The Single Best Investment: Creating Wealth with Dividend Growth by Lowell Miller. Published by Print Project 2006

The Ultimate Dividend Playbook: Income, Insight and Independence for Today's Investor by Josh Peters. Published by Wiley 2007

The Dividend Rich Investor: Building Wealth with High Quality, Dividend-Paying Stocks by Joseph Tigue & Joseph Lisanti. Published by McGraw-Hill 1998

Double Your Money in America's Finest Companies by Bill Staton. Published by Wiley 2008

The Dividend Growth Investment Strategy by Roxann Klugman. Published by Kensington Publishing Corp. 2001

Beating the S&P with Dividends, by Peter O'Shea and Jonathan Worrall. Published by John Wiley & Sons 2005

The Strategic Dividend Investor, by Daniel Peris. Published by McGraw-Hill 2011

About the author

My wife Raelene and I are retired and we are both in our late 70s. I consider myself an average investor. I've made a lot of novice mistakes over the years and learned from them as well. I do not consider myself an investing guru. That distinction would best describe Tom Connolly, who has published *The Connolly Report* for 37 years, since 1981. I have been a loyal follower and consider Tom a friend and mentor.

I have achieved what I consider financial freedom by following the Income Investment strategy. Our success may not be exactly what you wish to achieve, as everyone has different goals and requirements, but I hope I can provide some inspiration to seriously contemplate adopting this investment strategy.

We do not have a company pension. We live off our government pension and our dividend income. Currently our dividends exceed our living expenses, so we are able to reinvest approximately 60% of our profits to continue to grow our retirement income stream.

I hope that you have enjoyed learning about my investment strategy, and I would appreciate any comments or feedback. I wish you all the best with your own investment journey and if you would like to contact me directly email me at:

HMyourgrowingincome@gmail.com

Join me on my blog:
https://risingyieldoninvestments.blogspot.com/